THE
FEMALE
LEAD

THE FEMALE LEAD

WE RISE BY LIFTING OTHERS

BY EDWINA DUNN

ORIGINAL PHOTOGRAPHY BY
SANE SEVEN

IMPRESS—PUBLISHING

Published in 2021 by Impress-Publishing
www.impress-publishing.com

Impress-Publishing,
32 East Street,
Oxford OX2 0AU

Every woman in the book was interviewed on film.
These videos can all be seen at
www.thefemalelead.com

A CIP catalogue record for this book is available
from the British Library

ISBN 978—1—912930—79—1

Designed and typeset by Prof. Phil Cleaver
and Eilidh Doig of *et al design consultant*s
Print management by DLM Creative
Printed in Great Britain by Geoff Neal
and bound by Diamond Print Services

CONTENTS

WE RISE BY
LIFTING OTHERS
IS AT THE
HEART
OF WHAT WE ARE
DOING HERE.
WE DON'T LOSE A SINGLE
THING BY
SPEAKING UP FOR
ANOTHER
GIRL OR WOMAN.

EDWINA DUNN

We understand our world through stories; they form our culture and our history. For too long women have played supporting parts in these narratives, but in this book, women are centre stage.

In 2017, we launched our first book profiling 60 remarkable women. It was a celebration of their achievements and diversity, showing how women shape the world, providing positive role models for future generations.

This, our second book, reflects a different time. While the world has become more aware of persistent gender inequality, women in 2021 face unprecedented challenges post pandemic. Women are looking for answers to big questions and guidance on how to navigate our new future. Prior to writing this book we launched a study into women at work, to explore the barriers and persistent problems in the workplace and at home. What we discovered formed many of the questions put to the women in this book. Our interviews addressed some of the most pressing concerns about women's lives in 2021.

Each woman spoke to us directly. They were generous and open, often sharing deeply personal experiences. While telling their own stories they were frequently looking at the bigger picture and the uncertain future ahead. But *'uncertainty'* was not necessarily seen as negative; for with uncertainty can come the opportunity for change, and change was on the minds of all the women profiled. They talked about the need for change in every part of our society, to ensure a safe and equal world for women. These conversations were full of hope, but with the understanding that there must be a commitment to action; for every person to play their part in shaping a better world.

We rise by lifting others is our title, an important sentiment woven throughout the stories; the women spoke again and again about the need for a collective effort to make positive change. Not just for women, but for everyone. While they cared passionately about the global picture, at the heart of their stories was a search for personal fulfilment and purpose. The Female Lead is on a mission to help women find fulfilment and realise their personal goals, whatever they may be. We have designed online tools to give women the chance to examine their lives in the essential areas of self, work, money, relationships, and society. These five pillars are the framework for this collection and all of our women's stories relate back to them.

At the end of every interview, we asked the woman to select an object of significance in her life, and to explain her choice. Many picked an item with symbolic value associated with their sense of self; others chose items that summed up their professional life. Often the object reminded them of family and connection to others. This need for belonging and communion seemed ever more in their minds after a time when so many of us were separated from our loved ones during the pandemic.

Through the collected stories on these pages, we hope above all to show young women the countless routes to fulfilment. Together our female leads, who range in age, background, career, nationality, race, and beliefs, demonstrate that no one journey is right or successful. They are living proof that we must find our own paths and question the traditional options that women have been granted until now.

EDWINA DUNN

Edwina Dunn, a pioneer of big data, began her working life at the UK branch of CACI (Californian Analysis Centres Inc), and had risen to vice-president when she moved on to found Dunnhumby with her husband and colleague Clive Humby in 1989. Dunnhumby became a global big data force, bringing radically new capabilities to businesses around the world by using customer data to understand and predict consumer trends and behaviours. One of its notable successes was the Tesco Clubcard loyalty scheme, and the business was sold to Tesco in 2011. Edwina then joined global social media discovery engine Starcount as Chair. She is currently Deputy Chair of the Centre for Data Ethics & Innovation. In 2015, Edwina founded The Female Lead, which developed from the *What I See Project*, and launched in 2017. The Female Lead has since expanded to become one of the top five global campaigns for female empowerment. Edwina was appointed OBE in 2019 for services to data and business.

I've always been interested in what motivates people. That has been my work – I've always studied consumers and their behaviour. Outside work, I wanted to do something more creative. My initial idea was to explore what women see when they look in the mirror: that concept was the *What I See Project*. Women came up with completely different ideas: around half would talk about their physical characteristics, around half would explore questions like *'Who am I? What do I stand for?'*

I then thought of making a film, but I realised I wanted to go back to what I know – which is the facts. I decided I would interview woman and ask for their stories. Put really simply, this is about visible role models – no airbrushed lives, but real women, doing real things, in the world today. When I was younger, most leaders and charismatic characters were men; my role model back in the day was Red Adair, the oil well firefighter. I was modelling myself on men because there were no women.

With our first book, I thought we were creating a book of amazing women to inspire young girls. I thought we would produce the book, it would go into schools, girls would see real-life role models and that would be hat. But it became a whole lot more.

We started hearing about Female Lead societies, where girls were running their schools based on the principles of *The* Female Lead, and getting messages saying: *'This has changed how I think.'* It spurred me on to think we were doing something remarkable, though it's a very gentle project – we don't ever say one woman is better than another woman, it's gentle in the sense that it's *'make of this what you will.'*

I have circled back to technology: we are now bringing content to women on an online platform where women and girls can go to think, to be inspired, to find content that might help them in a moment when they need inspiration, succour, learning, or something to make them better or stronger. That has become my focus.

If women cannot advocate for other women, we should be ashamed.

And it isn't just girls who are inspired: it is women of all ages. Women whose lives are overwhelming them: women who have been told *'you can have it all, but you have to manage it all.'* Be careful what you wish for! Women have been given the opportunity to become superwomen, but there are no superwomen. It's such a horrible ambition for young women: that sense that you can have it all, and the feeling that you are inadequate if you don't quite manage it.

We are publishing this second book, quite simply because the appetite for these true stories is greater. While the stories in the first book remain current and relevant, because they are stories of women's real lives, we wanted to keep our investment in telling women's stories current. And we're also addressing some of the questions and issues that we have revealed through our own research.

These issues have been highlighted even more by Covid-19. The reality, of course, is that working from home isn't the same as flexible working, when you layer in the mental load in addition to the workload. It has created an extra burden.

The Female Lead is a platform where women and girls can go to think, to be inspired, to find content that might help them in a moment when they need inspiration, succour, learning, or something to make them better or stronger.

In our own primary research, something else that Covid-19 brought to the fore is that we all suddenly understood that we've all come to rely on the numbers. The world is becoming increasingly familiar with the idea that people will form policies and strategies based on data. The power of using data to present the facts around women is that we are more likely to win over leaders who are men. The more we can say these are the facts, rather than these are the emotions, the more likely we

are to win the day. Stories and anecdotes are still really important, but if we can say: this applies to 100 women, or 1,000 women, or 10,000 women, it becomes impossible to argue with. If you bring data to your argument, it makes a difference to that argument.

The purpose of our survey was essentially to measure fulfilment, using long-established psychological principles. We grouped our results into five pillars.

Self
When am I feeling enjoyment, satisfaction, energised, calm? What are the things that matter to me, versus the things that matter to the people around me? What's really interesting is how hard it is to imagine that someone else's motivations can be completely different to our own. Some people like to-do lists and getting things done; some people like to please others; some like to feel they've done something for a cause.

Society
As soon as we mention society, issues feel less under our control and therefore less meaningful, as though they are out of our hands. Saving the planet, going plastic-free, the gender division, the diversity division: what is our individual part to play, how much does it matter? I don't think that's been made real enough yet.

Work
Here we found a number of myths. There is a myth that women are not ambitious: in fact, they confidently say they are ambitious. There is a myth that when women have children, they become less committed. There is a myth that when women reach a certain age, they become less committed. This creates an expectation bias and a way of sidelining women, which causes them to falter mid-career. There is a myth that women don't like taking risks; they will take risks if they judge it worthwhile. Impostor syndrome: yes, women feel this. But it's not necessarily a bad thing

– it may mean that they work harder, they fight harder, they care more. It is important to challenge myths. It is also important to question whether women feel they are getting as far as they deserve and getting paid what they need. Promotion and salary structure is very opaque.

Relationships

If women want to have a completely fulfilled working life, how do they also have a fulfilled family life and fulfilling relationships? If women want to be treated equally, what happens in the home? One of the most defining features of women's success is their choice of partner. If their partner is willing to meet them half way – truly half way – they can fly. Expectation of relationships is so high in comparison to the reality, particularly in terms of childcare and elder care.

This is about visible role models – no airbrushed lives, but real women, doing real things, in the world today.

Money

We find that women look after the household money and the day-to-day – food on the table, the mortgage, the rent – but not investments or pensions. We are not used to talking about it, and it's tragic we often end up with the smaller pensions. Women are slower to invest and end up underinvested – they not only earn less but they have lower pensions and they live longer.

It's often suggested that women don't always help each other – that there's a kind of fear that, if they help other women, it will damage their own success, achievements, growth. This isn't the evidence that we see. Madeleine Albright has frequently said that there is a special place in hell for women who don't help other women. She's right. If women cannot advocate for other women, we should be ashamed. We rise by lifting others is at the heart of what we are doing here. We don't lose a single thing by speaking up for another girl or woman. And if we do that, all the talk around mentors and sponsors and role models would disappear – because we'd all be doing it.

Edwina's object

Samurai swords have captured my imagination. It really moves me that these swords are a sign of such loyalty to the samurai and to the lords that they served, and a symbol of their sense of honour and their allegiances. A samurai sword is a lethal weapon, but the Japanese have fought hard for the swords to be recognised as works of art. They are incredibly beautiful. The really old swords, from the 11th or 12th century, each have a unique pattern on the blade, telling when it was made and how it was used – almost as though they have an autograph. The craftsmanship and the masters who make them are revered. I was reading about them, learning about the blades and the smelting process, at the time when everything Clive and I were doing was about loyalty, and it felt kind of special that the whole concept of loyalty came from Japanese dynasties from so long ago.

SANDY POWELL

This is passing that generosity on. It's giving back.

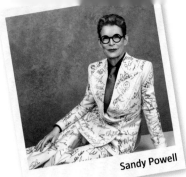
Sandy Powell

Billie Por

WE RISE BY LIFTING OTHERS

In the first Female Lead book we profiled Sandy Powell, legendary British costume designer and winner of three Academy Awards and three BAFTAs. In our original interview Sandy spoke about her mentor Derek Jarman who provided her first movie job and worked with her on four more films. In 1986 Jarman bought Prospect Cottage in Dungeness, UK. This became his home and an artwork in its own right. After his death in 1994, the cottage was cared for by his companion Keith Collins, who died in 2018. With the future of Prospect Cottage in the balance, The Art Fund aimed to raise £3.5m to protect its status as a museum and hub for young artists, and they succeeded. Sandy played a vital role, by turning a plain calico suit into a valuable piece of art, which she auctioned for the fund. By bringing together the most significant names in the film industry, she raised awareness and helped to reach the charity's target. The suit is now part of The Female Lead, who purchased it at the auction and it is a tangible symbol of our belief that 'we rise by lifting others'. The suit is the embodiment of a collective effort to make a difference and an expression of 'paying it forward'; the signatories helped to save Jarman's cottage, and that cottage will in turn help the next generation of artists as an inspiring place for them to work. Jarman nurtured new talent, like Sandy, and with that generous spirit he paid his success forward. And like the signatures on the suit, the women profiled in this book have come together to tell their stories, to inspire women of the future, to honour the women on whose shoulders we stand, and to encourage all women, individually and systematically, to keep on helping each other.

The story behind this suit goes back to February 2020 when I was lucky enough to receive both a BAFTA nomination and an Academy Award nomination. After the initial exhilaration my next thought was what to wear. I thought, *'I'm going to recycle'*. This white suit started out as a toile, which is a pattern for the suits my tailor made for me the year before. It's a blank canvas and I realised what an opportunity that would be to use it to make some money for the *Prospect Cottage* charity.

If we could save this house it would become almost a museum and a residence for young creatives to go and have somewhere inspiring to work.

Derek Jarman was the first director I ever worked with. He was my teacher and everything he taught me I still use today. He gave a lot of young people their first opportunity in the film industry. He was someone I looked up to and still do.

Initially I was just going to get the suit signed and put it up for auction, but I ended up going to lots of events where I would accost actors, directors, filmmakers and photograph them signing the suit. In total I got 200 signatures. There is Renee Zelweger, Margot Robbie, Robert De Niro, Brad Pitt, Joaquin Phoenix.

I was nervous about it being auctioned; it became part of me and I was possessive over it. I worried about it disappearing. When I found out that Edwina Dunn had bought it for The Female Lead I was thrilled. I know it's gone to a great home and we can use the suit again to raise money for The Female Lead – another fantastic cause.

The suit is completely about *'we rise by lifting others'*; it started out being about Derek Jarman, and without him I wouldn't be where I am today. He was such a generous soul and this is passing that generosity on. It's giving back.

FOREWORD

Dedicated to identifying and lifting barriers to women's fulfilment, The Female Lead amplifies the voices of women to ensure they impact culture, education and policy. The first volume showcased women's success across a range of fields; the second volume, without losing any breadth of women by age, nationality or ethnicity, focuses on specific themes in women's lives, such as childhood, family environment, goals and motivation. It provides a unique view of women's sense of self, their fit — or not — in society, the importance of relationships, what they hope to achieve and to change either in their own immediate lives or in the wider world, and how they have overcome impediments to their goals.

Every woman represented here is an achiever, but success is never the complete story. Each story also reveals experiences of failure and pockets of vulnerability. We hear about racism and its insidious mutability, often disguised but always felt. We hear about the joy of independence and self-efficacy, but we also hear about periods during which some women felt *'broken'*. We hear about trauma, whether from forced marriage or physical abuse, personal mistakes or unpredictable setbacks. We hear about dramatic turning points that require the reorganisation of identity and motivation. Sometimes these become emblematic lessons about obstacles and threats that women face more widely; sometimes they activate life-long values, such as the importance of speaking out and overcoming fear. We also hear about treasured objects, from teddy bears to trophies, and how each women imbues her *'special object'* with very personal meaning. And while we hear about apparent saviours who turn out to be tyrants, we also hear about the people who have supported and inspired them.

Every woman represented here is an achiever, but success is never the complete story.

The voices of these 67 Female Leads challenge some of the *'women are different'* myths and thereby complement what we learned about women's aims, goals and desires from the *Women at Work* project. Ambition is embraced without ambivalence or concern as to whether it is consistent with feminine norms. Imposter syndrome – the belief that you're not really as good as you seem, and that any moment your inadequacies might be exposed – was accepted as an inevitable feature of aiming high. It was not a barrier to achievement but a reminder that success and stature were not entitlements.

Each of these 67 women tells her own individual story, yet themes and narratives emerge that are distinctive to women very broadly. Adapting to circumstance, managing a range of obligations, stepping up to the needs of others (particularly to a child or parent) and dilemmas between a valued relationship, with either family or lover, and the requirements of self integrity are experiences that will resonate widely.

This new volume is a sharp reminder that standard measures of career success or personal achievement do not fit women's experiences.

As a psychologist working in life span development, I know that when these stories are read alongside comparable personal narratives of men, the differences are striking. There is seldom a single over-arching dream, as is often found in studies of men's development, nor are there blueprints or certainties that are common in men's life stories. When any of these 67 women's lives seems to have a simple unimpeded trajectory – for example, with youthful success and celebrity status – her own experience of that good fortune is shaped by the support she was given, the luck she had and her awareness that these are transient rather than secure. Women whose upward trajectory has been driven by brilliance or talent never see their rise as inevitable and always acknowledge others' help. No matter how remarkable and public their work and personna, the women insist on grounding themselves in everyday matters and relationships.

This new volume is a sharp reminder that standard measures of career success or personal achievement do not fit women's experiences. There is a restlessness, or dynamism, in their approach to personal fulfilment. They constantly seek new ways to combine and balance the many calls on their time, energy, interests and desires. They reveal a hunger for continued challenge and exercising new capabilities. The end of one phase of life leads to the question, *'What next?'* and, *'What is still to be done?'* or, perhaps, *'What aspects of my needs have I previously neglected?'*

How secure now is women's ability to explore and develop a wide range of options and do what they choose? In the first volume, written in 2015, women spoke optimistically about a fairer future. The outlook in this second volume is more cautious; the environment appears fragile, at risk from climate change, social division and upheaval. The pandemic crisis also looms as a reminder that progress is not necessarily permanent, and that a good life tomorrow is very dependent on the hard, well-informed work we do today. This important book showcases 67 women as they imagine a better future and whose stories provide a guide for tomorrow's women.

Terri Apter is a psychologist, writer and Fellow Emerita of Newnham College Cambridge. She has done a wide range of research on the hidden patterns of women's decision-making throughout their lives and the maze of challenges women confront in their careers. Her book *Altered Loves: Mothers and Daughters During Adolescence* was a New York Times *Notable Book of the Year* and *The Confident Child* was awarded the *Delta Kappa Gamma International Educator's Prize*. Her most recent book, *Passing Judgment: praise and blame in everyday life* highlights how daily exposure to praise and blame impacts on our relationships, from social media to marriage.
Dr Apter led The Female Lead's research into teen girls and social media for the *Disrupt Your Feed* campaign, and in 2020 joined forces with The Female Lead for the *Women at Work* Project.

BEING POSITIVE
DOESN'T MEAN YOU HAVE
TO BE HAPPY
OR COPE ALL THE TIME.
POSITIVE PEOPLE
CAN ACKNOWLEDGE ALL
THEIR EMOTIONS,
ARE STRONG ENOUGH
TO EXPERIENCE THEM ALL
AND TO BE VULNERABLE.

KATIE PIPER

SELF

Obstacles we find in ourselves. Celebrating the strength within.

The stories in this collection show the incredible strength, talent, ingenuity, resilience and bravery that women possess. Using the word *'inspiring'* to describe these women is an understatement. So many have beaten the odds to succeed in their fields of work; or broken free of the constraints of their individual circumstances. They are trailblazers. They are heroines. And we celebrate them all.

Women live with competing expectations from the world around them — to look perfect, to have successful careers, to be mothers, to get married, to be strong, but also nurturing. Building self-worth is complex when there is so much pressure to meet the societal standards of what it means to be a woman today.

If we can foster our sense of self, we can be empowered to define ourselves instead of being defined by society. If we can develop self-worth and confidence, we are able to show others how we should be treated and what we expect from them.

By looking within and developing self-awareness, we can grow in compassion for ourselves and others. We can find the inner strength that is there and create a rewarding life, as the women in this book demonstrate over and over again. But the starting point is always to take the lead in our own lives and to give ourselves the care and reflection that we all deserve to be fulfilled.

Knowing others is intelligence; knowing yourself is true wisdom. Mastering others is strength; mastering yourself is true power.
LAOZI

JULIA GILLARD

For me, a life lived in public is a by-product of the path I chose. I went into politics not to be a performer, but to get things done.

JULIA GILLARD

Julia Gillard was the 27th Prime Minister of Australia from June 2010 until June 2013; Australia's first, and so far only, female prime minister. In October 2012, she gave what has become known as *'the misogyny speech'* in the Australian parliament, the video of which has been viewed millions of times. In 2020, it was voted the most unforgettable moment in Australian TV history. Born in Barry, South Wales, Gillard emigrated to Adelaide with her family at the age of four. She is chair of the Australian mental health organisation Beyond Blue, chair of the Global Institute for Women's Leadership at King's College London, and chair of Wellcome. With Ngozi Okonjo-Iweala, she wrote *Women and Leadership*.

If my teenage self could see me now, I think she'd view what's happened as ridiculous. It's bizarre that a girl from Wales can migrate to Australia and end up being Prime Minister. I was never the class performer at school. I debated in high school but I was never the one right at the front. For me, a life lived in public is a by-product of the path I chose. I went into politics not to be a performer, but to get things done.

Shed your anxieties as early as you can, especially about the small stuff. Life is bigger than that.

My family was small and close-knit: me and my sister Alison, who's three years older than me; my father, who trained as a psychiatric nurse in Australia; and my mother, who worked as a cook in an aged-care facility. My father was a great believer in education. He'd done the 11 Plus exam and come third highest in all South Wales but, because of the poverty of his family, he had to leave school at 14 to work in the local shop.

When you come from a migrant family and your parents have missed out on opportunities you feel a special responsibility to live up to what they want for you. My family literally moved halfway around the world to give my sister and me a better chance in life. Interestingly, given that I grew up in the 1960s and 1970s, neither of my parents ever said

to us that we should limit our expectations because we were girls.

When I became Deputy Prime Minister and then Prime Minister, there was no missing the fact that I was the first woman in those jobs.

On my first day as Prime Minister, the media ran reports about what I was wearing rather than what I said. Female politicians are always asked about family structures – and there's no right answer. If you have kids, people ask who's looking after them and whether you can do a big job. If you don't have kids, and I don't, people wonder whether you really understand family life. But the essence of politics is you've got so much to do. There's not a moment to waste. You want to make the maximum amount of change you can in the time you are there. So I didn't dwell on it; I got on with the job.

When I gave what's come to be known as *'the misogyny speech'*, I had no idea it would resonate outside the parliamentary chamber, let alone that we'd still be talking about it all these years later. I think the speech has come to represent for many women a sort of battle anthem. It keeps finding a new audience because, unfortunately, women still have to navigate a very sexist world.

The rhythms of politics have been built around men's rather than women's lives. And then there are all the sexist stereotypes that swirl in our heads about women leaders. Many of the women Ngozi Okonjo-Iweala and I talked to for our book were conscious of being on a tightrope. If they came across as too tough, people would think, *'oh, she doesn't seem very likeable.'* But if they came across as too kind and empathetic, people would think, *'she seems nice, but she clearly lacks the backbone for the job.'* I do think this leads to a set of self-limiting behaviours; women leaders live with that voice in their heads telling them to be careful about their behaviour.

The best life advice I've been given was from a man called Alan Milburn, who served in Tony Blair's government. When I became Prime Minister, he rang to congratulate me and recommended I find the time to sit by myself and write down what my purpose was. I carried that sheet of paper with me during the years I was Prime Minister, and, on the toughest days, I'd get it out and it would steady me. It's advice I've often shared since. Ask yourself, *'what is the purpose of my life?'* and write it down.

My other piece of advice is probably to shed your anxieties as early as you can, especially about the small stuff. Life is bigger than that. Try to shed anxiety about appearance. Obviously, all of us care a bit about how we look but, as women, I think we're taught to worry about it far more than we should. Shed that anxiety and try to use the saved energy for things that are more meaningful.

On my first day as Prime Minister, the media ran reports about what I was wearing rather than what I said.

The gendered aspects of the attacks on me when I was Prime Minister did get very nasty from time to time. At rallies, people held up signs referring to me as a *'bitch'* or a *'witch'*. There was a radio commentator, a shock jock, who said I should be put in a bag and dropped out to sea. I got through those things by

reminding myself of my purpose – which was why it was so useful to have it written down – and by averting my eyes. I didn't sit there at night doomscrolling.

I'd seen women in politics get on a rollercoaster where they felt better about themselves after a day of good headlines and worse after a day of bad headlines. I'd decided that I wasn't going to do that. I wouldn't let myself be hijacked. I was going to be the same person whatever.

In my final speech as Prime Minister, I said I believed it would be easier for the next woman to become Australian Prime Minister, and I still do. In New Zealand, which is one of the two countries on earth to have had three women leaders, the Prime Minister Jacinda Ardern is very clear her experience is different thanks to the women who have gone before. And that gives me a lot of optimism. If we can keep battling through, it will get easier and easier for the women yet to come.

Julia's object
My object is my battered Aussie passport, which has been used so much in recent years. It represents the transition from my life as Prime Minister and the years before in Australian domestic politics, to the life I lead now, which still has many ties to Australia but involves working in other parts of the world. Obviously, the passport gets me around; for me personally, it represents the new life I lead now.

MEGAN CRABBE

*Often, we grab onto things we can
control as a way of feeling we have
power over the messy stuff. For me,
that was my body.*

MEGAN CRABBE

Megan Jayne Crabbe is a bestselling author, digital creator and presenter with more than 1.3 million followers across her social channels. She built her online platform creating content around the topics of body positivity, eating disorder recovery, mental health and feminism. In 2017 she wrote her first book, *Body Positive Power*, a manifesto on all the reasons why we hate our bodies, and how to change that. Megan has delivered talks, panels and presentations to audiences of thousands, and been a featured speaker at events hosted by Spotify, Instagram, Stylist Magazine, The Sunday Times, The Body Shop and more. In 2019 she co-created and toured a sell-out live show called *The Never Say Diet Club*, filled with empowering talks, comedy musicals, over-the-top dance numbers and lots of costume changes. She's also worked with the BBC, The Brits and Channel 4 as a presenter and podcast host.

I struggled with eating disorders until I was 16. After that I dieted. I didn't escape from everything being about my body until I was 21 and found the body positive movement. I was scrolling through Instagram one day looking at Fitspo and supermodels, and I found the opposite: a bunch of people finding happiness in something other than what their bodies looked like.

Until then, I'd lived my whole life believing that there was only one way to be happy and good enough – and suddenly there were these people forcing me to ask: what if that wasn't true? If it was possible to find happiness and fulfilment by changing my body, how come it hadn't happened yet? I'd been every size under the sun. I'd done every diet imaginable. I'd changed and moulded myself, and it hadn't worked.

I grew up in a small seaside town in Essex. My family is incredibly supportive. My dad's a teacher and my mum's the most caring person I've ever met. I think they were the perfect team, really; I couldn't have asked for better parents. I have two siblings. My older sister is sassy as hell and says and does whatever she pleases. I'm part of her care team. She has cerebral palsy and we all take shifts with her. She's taught me a whole lot about not apologising for who I am. And I have a older brother, A-Jay, who is living abroad, also a teacher, taking after my dad.

At school, I was a goody-two-shoes, a perfectionist. I got straight As. I'd do my homework early and ask for more. I can't deal with getting into trouble. I wish I'd had a little bit more rebel inside me. I wanted to sing, dance, perform, be on stage. In my teenage years, struggling with body image and eating disorders, I lost belief in myself. I didn't think it was possible for me to perform. I've somehow found my way back into a career that involves holding a mic and being centre stage, so it did work out, just not in the way I thought it would!

> *If it was possible to find happiness and fulfilment by changing my body, how come it hadn't happened yet?*

If my teenage self could see me now, she'd think: *'That's a lot of colours.'* I was queen of the emos. It was black everything, studded belts, fake lip piercing, you name it. She'd be shocked at the aesthetic. She'd love it secretly, but she wouldn't admit it. She wouldn't be able to believe that I've become a woman that thinks there's more to life than the body she has. I wish I'd been able back then to accept that life is messy. Often, we grab onto things we can control as a way of feeling we have power. For me, that was my body. I thought: *'If I can make this thing perfect then everything will be OK.'* I wish

I could have relaxed a bit more with the messiness and not felt as though I had to be in complete control.

Six years ago, body positivity wasn't as well-known as it is today. While I was finding out about it, I was using social media as a diary, recording what I was finding out about diet culture and fatphobia. My posts gained an audience, which led to me writing a book and doing podcasts, interviews, live shows, and a bit of presenting. It just snowballed. I don't want to tell people how to live or how to think; I want to give them the option to question our cultural standards, to say you're allowed to build a life that's about more than numbers and what you look like.

My career highlight so far isn't about me, it's about my sister. I got to be in a Little Mix video and my sister is the biggest Little Mix fan in existence. I kept it secret from her for months and arranged it that she came to the studio and was there when Little Mix walked into the room – and that moment, seeing her face, I'll never top that. For a long time, I was nervous about including my sister in my content. She's a huge part of my life and, as an adult, I've stepped into more of a carer role for her, so it seemed natural to include her. I was nervous about how people would react – if they'd see it as tactical. On social media, disabled people tend to be represented either as trauma porn or in terms of inspirational goals. We don't see multifaceted human beings. And my sister, who is a sassy little ball of fire, who can be a complete bitch sometimes, deserves to be seen. Plus she is just a bringer of joy.

I'm very aware that while I talk about beauty standards and fatphobia, I'm existing in a body that doesn't push people's ideas of beauty standards too far. I'm mid-to-plus-size. I'm mixed race but light-skinned. I want to acknowledge that for a lot of people I'm a palatable way into these movements. I hope people don't stop with me, that I'm a stepping stone to more radical body politics.

My social media is still polished. I still show up in my cutest outfit and take a hundred pictures before I post one. It's an interesting dilemma, critiquing the system while existing in it. You can only be seen and heard if you play the game, and the better you play it, the more you're seen and heard.

It's undeniable that social media has allowed people to question, learn, connect, find their people and their movements. But I'm terrified of the way it impacts our brains and how it encourages us to treat each other. The best advice I ever got was from Jes Baker, an incredible body liberation advocate and writer. She said: *'Megan, people aren't going to like you, and you will live.'*

The best feedback I've had hasn't come from my followers but from their parents. On the tour of our live show, the *Never Say Diet Club*, my best friend Joeley and I did meet-and-greets beforehand. So many young people showed up. We met, we hugged. It was lovely. And then the parents would take me to the side and say: *'I have my child back. They were gone for a long while and I didn't know how to reach them. And because of what you put out, I recognised them again.'* That is the best, most powerful response I could possibly get.

Megan's object
My significant object is a letter my dad gave me when I was 18, in which he said it wouldn't matter to him what I did professionally or where I chose to live or who I chose to love, he would always be proud of me as long as I acted with integrity. To him, that meant being true to my values, standing up for what I believe. I try to hold onto that when I'm not sure why I'm doing something or I'm facing a decision. The right thing is not always the easy thing or the thing that will make people like you.

JODIE WHITTAKER

*Go at your pace
and be you.*

JODIE WHITTAKER

Jodie Whittaker is a British actress who came to prominence in 2006, when she received the *Satellite & British Independent Film Award* nominations for her breakthrough role in the film *Venus*, written by Hanif Kureishi. Whittaker was only a few months out of the *Guildhall School of Music and Drama* and was so convincing in the audition that Kureishi and director Roger Michell changed the part from a Londoner to a northerner just for her. After leaving drama school in 2005 she worked steadily and appeared in *The Night Watch, Attack the Block, Black Mirror, Trust Me* and *Broadchurch*. In 2017 she made history by becoming the first woman to be The Doctor in *Doctor Who*, a role only played by men for the last 60 years. Whittaker appeared in her first full series as The Doctor in the eleventh series, which premiered in October 2018. She continued in the role in the twelfth series in 2020. Whittaker later announced that she would reprise her role as The Doctor into its thirteenth series.

I grew up in a village called Skelmanthorpe in Yorkshire. There were only the four of us in my family and we were really close. My ambition as a child was always to be an actress, even before I could articulate it. I'm a 1982 baby so I was blessed with a decade of incredible cinema that the whole community could enjoy. From the second the kids slid down the waterslide in *The Goonies* and I realised that that was someone's job, I was sold.

I'm not a natural rulebreaker in any way, so at school I was always really good; if you told me to do something I'd do it. I was not an academic kid. I've always been emotionally intelligent, and I've always been encouraged to be adventurous, but my academic achievements weren't anything to write home about. Because I was enthusiastic and always supported, I think I generally had a really happy childhood.

I applied for Drama School and got into my first-choice school. I realised that this requires a dedication and a level of self-worth and self-awareness that you're not necessarily ready for. I was graduating from Drama School in 2005 when two job opportunities came up. I got a job at The Globe Theatre, and I got a debut feature. Without those two jobs I don't think I could be sat here. I was given a platform in a way that not every person graduating from Drama School gets. With those opportunities

it meant that I auditioned and met the right people that led to me being cast as the first female Doctor Who, which is my pinnacle.

It's an absolute pleasure because of what it means emotionally to me and what it meant politically to me. Being cast as the first female Doctor - it's already old news and that's why it's brilliant. I'm already one of two now. Girls thought they would only get to be in the Tardis with The Doctor, and now we realise we don't have to think like that.

My teenage self would be delighted that I didn't pursue a back up plan.

It's really exciting when young people find a role model in a character. Girls and boys absolutely adored The Doctor in whatever form. The Doctor still remained a hero to all but what's brilliant for the girls is that they suddenly had an active role in their role play of being that character.

I don't think the previous Doctors represented all male actors. If someone took a particular issue to the casting, it was about that actor whereas with me, I wasn't just Jodie Whittaker playing the part, I was representing actresses and women. If I was annihilated for my interpretation of the role, I could have a really detrimental effect on us in the future and that was a massive amount of pressure.

If I could give any advice, it would be to celebrate you.

My teenage self would be delighted that I didn't pursue a backup plan. My mum and dad never encouraged one, but there were a couple of suggestions from other people that maybe wanting to be an actor wasn't necessarily a sensible thing to do. I didn't listen to that, and I had this really great support at home. I had parents who said, '*do it*' and don't worry about a backup plan until your first plan doesn't work out. Don't spread your energy.

I'm so chuffed that I listened to that advice. I would tell my teenage self, '*You're not going to grow out of the anxiety, but you'll get better at dealing with it.*' I still feel as stressed and anxious as I did when I was 14, but life has given me coping mechanisms. I'm not flawless but I've got better at it. I've learned to deal with the noise.

The best life advice I've ever received is from my dad who said, '*If you don't ask, you'll never know*', so I've never been embarrassed to say I don't understand. I didn't realise that not everyone is blessed with that kind of confidence.

If I could give any advice, it would be to celebrate you. That sounds like something you might find on the inside of a card, but it's really hard when you don't feel like you fit in. Don't give up. You have a long life, and you go at your pace and be you.

The living woman who most inspires me is my mum. She had me in her early thirties and I was really lucky to be brought up by someone who, without realising it, is incredibly

progressive, incredibly nurturing, incredibly loyal and non-judgemental. I realise those are not easy things to achieve as an adult or as a human. Without that I wouldn't have achieved anything. She takes up no space but is the brightest light in a room for me.

Jodie's Object
I've got a pair of my nephew's pyjamas. Those are my most treasured things because they will forever remind me of him. Some of us are lucky enough to get older whereas some of us live short but beautiful lives. Whatever is happening in life, there is a fragility and honour in being alive. We should never take those things for granted.

NITA AMBANI
Photography by Reliance Foundation

We are where we are thanks to the fearless and relentless struggles of generations of women before us.

NITA AMBANI

Nita Ambani is an educationist, philanthropist, businesswoman, patron of arts and sports, and champion of women and children's rights. Through the various initiatives of Reliance Foundation, of which she is founder and chair, she seeks to empower women in India with resources and opportunities. On International Women's Day 2021, she launched an inclusive and collaborative digital movement for women called *Her Circle*. She is the owner of Mumbai Indians, the most successful cricket team in the Indian Premier League, the founder chairperson of Football Sports Development Limited, which launched the Indian Super League, and the head of the *Education and Sports for All* initiative for children. Through Sir H N Reliance Foundation Hospital and Research Centre in Mumbai, she is committed to making affordable world-class medical care available to all Indians. US magazine Town and Country recognised her as one of the world's top philanthropists in 2020, and Fortune India has ranked her as *India's Most Powerful Woman*.

I grew up in a small suburb of Mumbai called Santacruz, in what we call a *'joint family'* in India, with all my aunts and uncles, surrounded by cousins; 11 girls and one boy. We were raised to believe that we could achieve anything we wanted – no goal was too big, no dream impossible. I loved my large family and I was shaped by the strong value system that they ingrained in all of us.

It was my father's kindness and empathy that shaped me into who I am today. He taught me the most precious principle of life; the ability to care. Another formative memory is of one of my eldest uncles, who was visually impaired. He chose me to read newspapers and books to him every day. The reading would be followed by discussions in which he would encourage me to express my points of view. Even as a child, my opinion mattered. That instilled a lot of confidence in me. It also showed me that caring for others is deeply joyful and rewarding, and that each one of us can help in making a difference for the better in the life of others. I think, as women, and individuals, the freedom to have opinions gives us a level of confidence that can pave the course of our lives.

My earliest role models were the amazing women in my family, starting with my courageous and ever-optimistic mother, my Gandhian grandmother, and my incredible aunts, who were all pathbreaking in their time as swimmers, teachers, and freedom fighters in the movement for India's independence. These women taught me compassion and resilience. After I got married, I was inspired by my father-in-law, Dhirubhai Ambani, who from being a fuel attendant went on to build an industrial empire from scratch, and my husband, Mukesh Ambani, who has always encouraged me to believe in my dreams.

I think, as women, and individuals, the freedom to have opinions gives us a level of confidence that can pave the course of our lives.

Working with children was always my calling. I trained as a teacher after my marriage and started working in a primary school. When Mukesh was setting up a manufacturing site in Patalganga, a huge industrial hub in Navi Mumbai, my father-in-law asked me to set up a school there. And there on, wherever Mukesh started a factory, I started a school! Today, I am overjoyed to be running 14 schools, educating over 78,000 students so far. Nothing gives me more joy than the sight of happy children in a classroom or playground.

I was 44 when sport came into my life and gave me a whole new perspective and world view. We owned the Mumbai Indians (MI) team in the Indian Premier League, and for two years MI had been at the bottom of the table. In season two, I flew to South Africa to motivate and be with the team. That's how it all started in 2009 – from those first team meetings, learning nitty-gritties of the game, living and breathing cricket every single moment! Mumbai Indians is now the most valuable team in the IPL and the only one to have lifted the trophy five times! As women's cricket gets more structured, competitive, and engaging, I am sure the day is not far off when we will also have women's cricket teams in the IPL.

I think it's a blessing to be a woman, in any era or age. We are where we are thanks to the fearless and relentless struggles of generations of women before us. So, we owe it to future generations to keep pushing boundaries. There is so much still to achieve. Equal representation and equal pay are important conversations today in every field, be it sport or politics or art or science. Young girls all over the world must be encouraged and supported to follow their dreams. When women have goals and aspirations, they positively impact their families and communities. Through our work at Reliance Foundation, we have seen that every time a woman does well for herself, she has the power to open opportunities for other women too.

Reliance Foundation is the philanthropic arm of Reliance Industries. It was started to formalise what was already a way of life for us – to do good for as many people as possible. With around half of India's population, over 600 million Indians, being under the age of 25, we believe wholeheartedly in the power and potential of our youth. Through Reliance Foundation, we want to enable and empower all Indians with access, infrastructure, and opportunity so they can dream big dreams and make them all come true. Our aim is to spread hope across the length and breadth of our country, especially amongst the most marginalised and vulnerable communities.

The COVID-19 pandemic has affected all of humanity, inflicting unimaginable despair and uncertainty all over the world. As it spread across continents, our first thought was to do whatever we could to safeguard our people, throughout our country as far and wide as we could. It was not just our collective and patriotic duty, but also our moral and human responsibility towards one another. Within days of the outbreak, Reliance Foundation set up dedicated COVID hospitals treating thousands of patients free of cost. We ran the world's largest free meal distribution programme by a corporate foundation. Every life is precious, and every little act of care and positivity makes a difference. I am an eternal optimist – I believe that together we can and we will overcome this crisis and every challenge that comes our way.

Nita's Object
My object is my wedding saree, a traditional gajji silk drape that was handwoven by local artisans in the same community where my mother's and her mother's wedding outfits were woven. What makes my wedding saree even more special for me 36 years down the line is that my daughter Isha chose to wear the same drape on her wedding day. It is the perfect embodiment of the unconditional love that passes down as blessings to the next generations.

MAYA GHAZAL

*I work every day to give back to the
country that has welcomed me.*

MAYA GHAZAL

Maya Ghazal is a Goodwill Ambassador for UNHCR, the United Nations Refugee Agency. In 2015, she fled Damascus and started a new life in the UK under a family reunification scheme. She went on to study for a degree in Aviation Engineering and Pilot Studies at Brunel University London. At 21, Maya became the first female Syrian refugee pilot, and she plans to work as a commercial airline pilot. The recipient of the *Princess Diana Legacy Award* in 2017, she advocates for refugee inclusion, access to education and job opportunities, and counters negative stereotyping. She has spoken at events all over the world including *WE Day*, the *WISE Summit*, and the first ever *Global Refugee Forum* in 2019.

I grew up in Damascus. Life was normal: we'd watch Disney and Hannah Montana was a favourite. I didn't come from a rich family but we were comfortable – we had cars and we'd go on holiday once a year. We'd see our grandparents every week and I had many friends. The Syria I remember was happy and colourful and filled with life. It was not what you see on TV.

The civil war, which started in 2011, made life so different. Necessities like water, electricity and gas were difficult to get hold of and normal life was not possible. My parents knew that education was the key for us to succeed but, after a few years, it became dangerous for us to go to school. My dad made the decision to leave my country for the UK and, after 15 months, he managed to apply for family reunion visas and my mother, my two younger brothers and I joined him. As we had visas, we travelled by plane.

I had to start from zero at the age of 16 and it was hard.

I miss my country so much. I miss the person that I was. Coming to the UK changed me; I had to learn a new language and adapt to the culture. I had to start from zero at the age of 16 and it was hard. My English was very limited and I found it hard to communicate with people.

When I first arrived in the UK, I could see stereotypical expectations. People would say,

'How was your journey?' and I was a huge disappointment because I didn't have juicy adventures to talk about: I didn't come to the UK by sea.

Going to school in Syria had often been a life and death situation, but I had worked really hard to achieve my qualifications and managed to complete the equivalent of GCSEs. I was very proud that I got As, and my worst grade was a B in French. When I visited schools, I told them about my ambitions to study hard and go to university. But, as soon as they knew I was Syrian, they thought that I was someone who was not educated, who had lived in a tent and come here illegally. I felt hurt. They didn't give me a chance to tell them who Maya Ghazal was. I got rejected by three schools. One of them didn't even agree to see me, they gave me a sticky note with the address of my council and said, 'They will sort you out.'

That crushed me at the time, but, looking back, it made me who I am today. It made me value education even more. I taught myself English and managed to get a place at college and proved that I was not stupid; I could sit in a classroom with people my age and understand and achieve.

I first got the idea of becoming a pilot when I stayed in a hotel by Heathrow airport. I could see the runway and the planes taking off and landing and I was fascinated. I said to my mum, 'This is what I want to do, I want to control those planes.'

So many people said that I would not make it in such a field. I got told that, because I'm Muslim, Arab and female, nobody would give me a job – it would be a major security issue. I knew this was just talk and that I needed to get going, so I applied to study Aviation Engineering at university. Last August, I earned my private pilot's licence and I am very close to graduating from university. No matter what people say, as long as you believe in your abilities, you can move mountains.

What I love about flying is that, literally, the sky is the limit. As a pilot, I will travel from country to country. I was once rejected by countries because of my nationality but, because of my job, I will be welcomed. The best moment in my training was the first time my instructor said, *'The plane is yours, you can fly by yourself.'* He spoke to the control tower to change the captain details and it gave me goosebumps to hear my name as pilot-in-command.

As long as you believe in your abilities, you can move mountains.

People talk about 80 million refugees worldwide. Those aren't just numbers, those are the lives and futures of people who've sacrificed everything. Being displaced from our country doesn't mean that we lose our humanity – we still have dreams and hopes. We are not here to take jobs or money. I appreciate the second chance that I have been given and I work every day to give back to the country that has welcomed me.

I want people to understand that it doesn't take much to make someone's life better. The smallest act of kindness makes a difference. For me, someone telling me that my English sounded good made me believe in myself again. She was a volunteer manager at a charity called The Children's Society.

It was in June 2015 and I spoke at one of their youth clubs. The manager made me believe in myself, she raised my confidence and without her I wouldn't be the same. I literally couldn't speak English and now I am invited to give speeches around the world to inspire others.

The war in Syria will end at some point and, when it does, I will go back and help rebuild. I hope it will become a proper country again. But, eventually, I will come back to the UK. I feel it is my home now.

Maya's object
A teacher in Syria gave me this notebook. I started writing in it when we came to the UK. I was not going to school because I kept getting rejected and told my English was terrible. But I wasn't going to let my lack of English stop me. I wrote down every single word that I didn't understand, which was 99 per cent of what I heard. Every line of the notebook is filled with English adjectives, verbs and nouns. First, I would write the word phonetically using the Arabic alphabet and then I would use a dictionary to look up the meaning of the word and write it in English. After six months of continuous use, I started at college. This notebook symbolises my journey.

KATIE PIPER

I want to get to a point where visible difference stops being a talking point. I don't want to be talking about this in 10 years' time.

KATIE PIPER

Katie Piper is a best-selling author, TV presenter and philanthropist. Described as an *'icon of her generation'*, Katie secured her place in the nation's hearts when she appeared on Channel 4's BAFTA nominated documentary *Katie: My Beautiful Face*, which covered the early stages of her recovery after an acid attack in 2008. For over a decade, Katie has devoted her life to The Katie Piper Foundation to support those living with burns and scars; she has received numerous awards, accolades and doctorates for her work. Katie is a much-loved presenter for the BBC's *Songs of Praise*, the host of the acclaimed *Katie Piper's Extraordinary People* podcast and face of iconic global beauty brands. Katie is dedicated to removing the traditional stigma of beauty across the media and will continue to lead thought promoting diversity, inclusion and acceptance across society.

At school I was bossy, headstrong, determined and not very academic. My school reports always said I talked too much – but that turned out to be a good thing. I grew up in Charlton, a small village near Andover in Hampshire, the middle one of three, wearing my older brother's clothes and playing with his toys. We spent our time out in the fields, climbing trees. There was no internet. Looking back, it was a pretty amazing childhood.

I'm now the mother of two young daughters. I try not to live through them. They need to have their own hopes and dreams. I want them to be robust and at the same time to know it's OK not to be strong all the time. We must be responsible for ourselves, carry ourselves through life, and that isn't about avoiding pain or hurt, which are inevitable.

My belief is that as a woman it's very important to be independent. I want my girls not to have to rely on other people to feel complete – so that anyone who comes into their life is a welcome addition rather than a necessity to complete them, or being something they're waiting for in order to become themselves.

At the Katie Piper Foundation, the charity I set up to support burns rehabilitation and scar management for UK survivors, there's the physical side of burns treatment and there's also a social and wellbeing side. After acute care, we help people rebuild their lives to the standard they want. It's not just about going back to normal, it's about empowering them to be whatever they want to be after their injury.

My long-term hope is that one day we won't be needed because burns and scars are accepted as a part of life, that they're not a reason to ostracise somebody or assume they're not up to the job when they come for an interview or find them unattractive because they're different and the media tells us that only symmetry is appealing.

I had to go abroad for my rehab, but with the Katie Piper Foundation we have our own rehab centre here in the UK now. The day we finalised it, I rang my mum and said: *'I can't believe we've done it. I can't believe that for the next girl and her mum, it's going to be different, that she will be able to come here for free and get access to treatment and support.'* It was a real wow moment.

There are so many brilliant conversations happening around diversity now. There are also some harmful ones – and if we're talking about disfigurement, specifically burn scars, there's so much more that we could be doing. We need to see more examples of people with visible difference doing normal, everyday things, not simply as part of a campaign but where the difference is incidental. We're scared of what we don't understand. I want to get to a point where visible difference stops being a talking point. I don't want to be talking about this in 10 years' time.

Working with people with unimaginable trauma has restored my faith in people's kindness, courage, and tenacity. The human spirit is strong. Ill bodies can be shattered and torn apart but there's something deep within us all that's indestructible, that can cope with the unthinkable and come back.

As a young girl, you can't be what you don't see.

Mindset is key. I'm not a fluffy person. Being positive doesn't mean you have to be happy or cope all the time. Positive people can acknowledge all their emotions, are strong enough to experience them all and to be vulnerable. I've had some euphoric moments in my life. I've had dark moments when I've questioned why this is happening to me or my family. And then there are other moments when things are dull. I like the idea that you breathe in through the amazing parts, hold on through the awful, and breathe out and relax during the ordinary parts.

I have a faith. I wasn't brought up a Christian, although my parents' values and morals were Christian: treat others how you want to be treated, love your neighbour. Later I joined a church and I'd go twice a week. My faith got me through when I felt I had nothing else left. Now that I'm a mum it's something I impart to my children, but I'll leave it up to them whether they want to carry it on when they're older.

My career now is so varied that I couldn't describe a typical day. The best thing is simply to be here, a woman living with a full facial burn. I'm an ambassador for Pantene. I couldn't imagine, when I was first burnt, seeing a shampoo advertisement featuring a woman who's blind in one eye, with her whole face skin-grafted. It would have completely changed how I felt about my appearance.

To exist authentically, not have to Photoshop my appearance, feels so, so good.

When I was first burnt, I remember thinking: *'How am I going to be me?'* The only people I've seen with burns are military. As a young girl, you can't be what you don't see, so when the beauty industry changes to be more inclusive, the effects are amazing and ripple on for years to come.

The pandemic and the lockdown reminded me to slow down and remember that the most valuable things are health and time because we can't get them back. Busy woman syndrome is a distraction, filling your life with activity. It can be about status – trying to show your worth through in demand you are – and it can be a response to trauma, a way of not dealing with underlying feelings.

I'm really into affirmations, and one of my favourites is: *'Worry is a total waste of time. All it does is steal your joy and keep you very busy doing absolutely nothing at all.'* There's no point in obsessing about things that haven't happened. The bad stuff that happened to me wasn't the stuff I'd worried about. I worried about other stuff – which shows what a waste of resources anxiety is.

Katie's object
My object is my graduation hat, because I didn't do A levels, I didn't go to university but, fast-forward all these years, I was recognised with an honorary degree from the Royal College of Surgeons in Ireland. That seemed a real moment of hope and achievement.

JADE THIRLWALL
Photography by Jordan Rossi

The older I get, the less I care; being around the right people helps.

JADE THIRLWALL

Jade Thirlwall is a singer-songwriter and member of Little Mix, the world's biggest girl band with over 60 million records sold, 10 billion global streams and 5 UK Number 1 singles; including BRIT Award winning *Shout Out To My Ex* (2016). In 2021, Little Mix became the first female band in the history of the BRIT Awards to win the award for British Group. Jade is a passionate ambassador and ally for Stonewall UK, a charity which stands for LGBTQ+ rights and people everywhere. Jade also works closely with UNICEF. Always wanting to give back and stay connected to the place where she grew up, Jade became Honorary President for her hometown football club South Shields FC in 2020 and is patron to local charity Cancer Connections. With bandmate Leigh-Anne Pinnock, Jade won the *Equality Award* at the Ethnicity Awards in 2020.

I grew up in South Shields, a small northern working-class town. My mam worked at my primary school as a business manager, my dad as a taxi driver. My dad's side of the family are white, my Mam is mixed; my Grandad was Yemeni, and my Nanna was Egyptian – she passed away when my Mam was little. It was a multicultural environment. My Grandad was keen on celebrating our heritage and cooking Yemeni food. We lived next to the mosque and 35 different languages were spoken at my school. I was shy and timid but I found that I could express myself on stage, singing and dancing. I always felt loved and protected growing up, especially by my Grandad, who was a beautiful person.

During my secondary years, there was a lot of bullying, my grandad passed away, and I developed an eating disorder.

The minute I went to secondary school things changed. I was the only person from my primary who went to my predominantly white Catholic secondary and, immediately, I had no friends and I was an easy target. My Mam sent me there because it was one of the best schools in the borough and she thought she was doing the right thing. During my secondary years, there was a lot of bullying, my grandad passed away, and I developed an eating disorder. I was given a school '*buddy*',

someone who would keep an eye on me and help me – it was through them that I met my best friend Holly. We've been inseparable since and live together now in London.

The first time I did *X Factor*, the show on which Little Mix was formed, I was 15 and I didn't want anyone to know. But the show sent a camera crew to my school and I had to stand on stage and say, '*I'm through to boot camp!*' I got sent home in the first week. It was humiliating and, as a teenager, the worst thing in the world. But, weirdly, being seen on telly scored me a few cool points at school.

The second time I did *X Factor*, I was 17. It was the year that One Direction were put together; there was a girl band called Belle Amie, but I didn't get in. The third time, I didn't actually want to go on *X Factor*. My older brother, who has always been a big champion of mine, said, '*Jade, just go. I know how much you want this, and you never know - third time lucky!*' So I went, I was put in Little Mix, and the rest is history.

We have been together 10 years and I find that we are still trying to prove ourselves. In the music industry, misogyny and sexism still exist. For a girl band, it's hard to be taken seriously and not constantly sexualised. One of the blessings of social media is that you can now be successful without having to beg a record label to sign you or having to listen to what sort of artist anyone else thinks you should be. Artists like Billie Eilish, who is so authentic, are inspiring for people like me who started in a different era of music for women. It is so important to stay true to yourself.

We got emotional when we won the *BRIT Award for British Group* because it wasn't just the award, it was the thought that, in 43 years of the BRITs, a girl band had never won. It's mind-blowing. In our speech it was important to acknowledge all the incredible girl bands that had come before – from Bananarama to Mis-Teeq and the Spice Girls; bands who are iconic in pop culture but were never given the recognition that they deserved. It was a big statement for us to say, *'Thank you very much for this award but it's about time.'*

I find it strange that people go on social media to say something negative and tag us – they want us to see it. I have turned my Instagram tags off and rarely go on Twitter: I've found that it's important for my mental wellbeing to not be on my phone too much. I have been guilty of typing my name into Twitter and looking for the worst someone can say about me, just to confirm the insecurity I was already feeling. That's toxic and, over the years, I have had to learn to stop. Stopping giving my energy to that negativity was the best thing I could have done.

The older I get, the less I care; being around the right people helps. Poetry is therapy. I sometimes struggle to express how I am feeling and a way of letting emotions out is by writing. Being in the public eye, if you have issues you often have to push them to one side. When the first lockdown happened, I was suddenly alone with my thoughts and took to writing. My boyfriend taught me a technique called future journaling where you write what you see for the future, all positive things, your ideals. I wrote my thoughts every night before bed and then started writing poetry and I felt this weight lifting.

If I could, I'd tell my teenage self to stop worrying. Being in a space where I was bullied for my skin colour, my ethnicity, my heritage, I battled over where I was meant to belong. Being biracial, I sometimes didn't feel white enough, I didn't feel black enough, I didn't feel Arab enough. On top of that I was skinny and spotty. I was desperate to change the way I looked to feel more accepted, and going into the music industry just added a magnifying glass to those feelings. I wish that I had been able to shake myself and say, *'Just be yourself. That wins every time.'*

Jade's object
My leavers' book from secondary school holds lovely memories. I live with my best friend from school now, and the first page is from her. There are nice pictures and she talks about how far I've come since I was anorexic. There are messages from friends saying, *'I hope you win X Factor'* and from teachers and a school counsellor I used to talk to. Every page is a lesson, as there are even messages with racial undertones from students who must have been my friends. There was a running joke that I was Arab, which I think I blocked out. It is good for me to remember that I went along with this stuff out of fear of not fitting in. It's a reminder to stand up for myself and to challenge those attitudes and behaviours.

SÔNIA GUAJAJARA
Photography by Jessica Mangaba

The fight for mother earth is the mother of all fights.

SÔNIA GUAJAJARA

Sônia Guajajara, is a Brazilian indigenous activist, environmentalist and politician. A member of the Socialism and Liberty Party (PSOL), she ran as a candidate for President of Brazil in the 2018 election, before being chosen as the vice presidential running mate of nominee Guilherme Boulos. She is the first indigenous person to run for a federal executive position in Brazil. She was born in the Amazonian rainforest and attended the Federal University of Maranhão, after which she worked as a teacher and a nurse. Guajajara is the leader of the Association of the Indigenous Peoples of Brazil, an organisation that represents around 300 indigenous ethnic groups. As an activist, she fights for the rights of indigenous people and against further development and deforestation of the Amazon Rainforest. Among her many honours she was awarded the *Order of Cultural Merit* from the Brazilian Ministry of Culture and the *Medal of Honor* of the Government of the State of Maranhão. Guajajara has participated in several United Nations Climate Change Conferences (COPs) and other international events, always representing indigenous causes, especially the demarcation of lands and the defence of human rights. In 2020, the Latinos por la Tierra group elected her one of the 100 most influential personalities in Latin America.

I'm from Araiboia, an indigenous territory in Amarante city, Maranhão state. My parents are illiterate. They never learned how to read, but the fact they can't read books does not mean they are ignorant. They have always been very wise and responsible. They wanted their children to study and their eight children got college degrees. I have always loved to study and always studied hard.

In preschool I would help the teacher with the other children. I believe that when it comes to being a leader you are born with the gift. You are born a leader and anywhere you are you can step up, be active, help fight for what is right. I have always been that kind of person.

My school was in a nearby village. The class was for indigenous and non-indigenous people. This was important because very often non-indigenous people know nothing about us and tend to avoid us. A lot of people treat us as inferior or incapable beings with a primitive and backward culture. In our school non-indigenous people grew up knowing that we are all human beings. That we are people.

If people can grow up knowing who you are they will support, defend and help you.

I guess I was born a political person. We always saw the indigenous movement as a political struggle. The fight for rights, the fight for respect, for justice; it is all a political struggle. I was a presidential candidate in 2019 and the first woman and indigenous person in that position in history. I wanted to confront the Brazilian state which had always denied our existence and our rights. We need to occupy positions where we can foster public debate about indigenous issues. Especially environmental issues, which have been completely neglected.

We must have indigenous people at all levels of political decision making; in local, state, and national spheres. But it is not a reality yet and there are still very few indigenous politicians and mayors.

In 2018 we had 130 indigenous candidates for the House of Representatives, the Senate and vice-presidency. It didn't matter what the election result was, what mattered to us was to have more visibility. We had to show that we can occupy any function in this country, after all, it is originally an indigenous country.

The indigenous fight and environmental fight can't be separated. It is a single fight because we are nature.

Sexism has become a natural behaviour in Brazil. It is a colonial legacy and is difficult to let go of and in indigenous territories it is no different, sexism is there too. For us this is a double challenge because although it is sexism people want to justify it as culture; a culture where women do not participate in certain spaces. So being an indigenous leader and woman is a huge challenge. It seems that only men's opinions matter; when women are talking they interrupt them. These are big challenges and we are going to overcome them.

In 2019 we organised the first march of indigenous women in Brazil. It was the first one in the world and we gathered almost 4000 women. Women came up to me and said: *'I want to be a leader. I want to have a role in organisations. I want to be a senator.'* So many women revealed this to me and now we have 44 women elected as councillors and vice mayors and even a mayor. The important thing is that we empower more and more women.

Indigenous rights are fundamental for the life of our planet. These rights ensure a balanced environment. The indigenous fight and environmental fight cannot be separated. It is a single fight because we are nature. For Brazil and for the world it is urgent to break with the current economic model based on large scale production, unrestrained mining, and the use of rivers for power plants. It is a

model that does not support itself. Studies now show what we have been saying for thousands of years; that nature is not infinite. Society must understand this.

Historically this environmental issue has been left aside in public debates and politics. Today the whole world can see how urgent this fight is. Indigenous people treat the land as a mother. That is why we care because for us it is Mother Earth. And a mother is taken care of, is protected, and not sold. The fight for mother earth is the mother of all fights.

Sônia's object

My object is the maraca. We use it to sing, to celebrate, to dance and it is used in all the festivals and rituals of our Guajajara people. For me it is the symbol of our fight, of our resistance, of our life of celebrations. Because if you do not have a voice, you can't scream, you can't be heard. You can suffocate in your own silence. So, for us the maraca represents that cry of life and resistance.

51

CHELSIE HILL
Photography by Rollettes

*I dance because I feel my so-called
limitation disappears.*

CHELSIE HILL

Chelsie Hill is an entrepreneur and founder of the Rollettes dance team. At the age of 17, she was a passenger in a drunk driving incident, which caused irreversible damage to her spinal cord and left her unable to walk. As a wheelchair user, she was determined to pursue her original ambition to dance. In addition to the Rollettes dance team, she is the founder of the *Rollettes Experience*, an annual weekend-long event bringing together women wheelchair users of all ages for dance, workshops, and seminars. Chelsie also continues her work with her mentorship program, *Boundless Babe Society* to build leaders in the community.

I grew up in Monterey, California, about six hours north of Los Angeles. I was always a dancer. I talked about being in music videos and being a backing dancer and going on tour. I had lots of friends at school but sitting down and having to concentrate was really hard for me. I always wanted to be doing something active.

In my senior year of high school, I was at a party. I was working the next morning, so I had to get home. All of us were drinking. Someone asked if anyone needed a ride — and, long story short, I climbed in the back seat. We passed my house and slowed down, and I had the opportunity to get out of the car. They offered to let me out and I said, *'No, it's fine, you guys can drop me off on the way back into town.'*

We ended up hitting a tree head-on, going about 35 miles per hour. I broke my back instantly. I woke up in hospital about two weeks later and the doctor said: *'Do you have any questions for me?'* I said, *'Yeah, why can't I feel my legs?'* Previously my family and friends had been telling me it was the medicine. They wanted to make sure when I heard the news that I was completely coherent. He said: *'Well, you have a spinal cord injury and you're never going to walk again.'*

The next thing I said to the doctor was, *'I don't just walk, I'm a dancer.'* He shook his head and said, *'I'm sorry, it's not possible.'* I was in disbelief the entire first year. My family were wonderful. When I said, *'Dad, I want to drive.*

I'm about to be 18 years old, I'm about to go to college, I don't want you and Mom to drive me for the rest of my life.', he threw me the keys and said: *'Alright, let's do this.'* It was always, *'Let's figure it out.'*

For a long time, I replayed the moment when my friends slowed down the car at the Stop sign and asked if I wanted to get out. That split-second decision completely altered my life. I had to forgive myself for making it, and to take responsibility for getting in the car knowing the driver was intoxicated. I didn't know how much he'd drunk: it could have been a sip — but no matter what the amount, it's never right. I needed to be able to own what I did and not blame someone else.

> *If I could change one thing, it would be the narrative, people looking at us like we're a charity.*

In hospital, I saw a video of a wheelchair dancer and it ignited something in me. My high school dance team wanted me to perform with them in the last rally of the year. My dad went around finding wheelchairs and my able-bodied team created a wheelchair dance team around me. I still had my back brace on — it was only about two months after I was paralysed — and we surprised my whole school. The feeling of dancing with people who were like me was so cool. I didn't feel different. I felt welcomed.

In a team, no one person is better than another. You're only as good as your 'weakest' person.

I wanted to meet other people I could do this with. I organised a weekend and I reached out on social media for girls who wanted to dance in wheelchairs to come and hang out. I hustled studios for discounted rates, and restaurants to give us free food, and hotels for rooms, and six girls flew in, and we had three days of dancing, went out to dinner, had sleepovers. And on our last night, we did a performance for my hometown and put videos online. And from there it exploded.

I moved to Los Angeles in 2014, four years after I was paralysed and two years after I started the dance team. That's what I'd wanted to do before my accident. It's where the best studios are. I knew I was good enough. I rolled into my first class in the best studio in Los Angeles and it was horrible. I wasn't confident and everyone crowded around, and I couldn't see, and I ended up leaving. I cried and cried.

It was so frustrating because I knew I was good. I knew how good I'd been when I was walking, and I knew how good I was as a wheelchair dancer. I knew I could adapt the choreography. And after three months, I tried again, at other studios.

I dance because I feel my so-called limitation disappears. I want to create dance videos showcasing my disability and normalising it. And there have been some great moments. The Rollettes were the first wheelchair dance team to perform at the Hollywood Christmas Parade. I had the chance to tell my story, and dance, on the Ellen show. And in 2018, we had the *Rollettes Experience*. I was with the team on stage, looking out at a ballroom of women and children dancing in wheelchairs. And if I die tomorrow, I could die happy because I was able to make that come true with the rest of the team.

There are plenty of people advocating for the disabled community, and there's so much that could be done for accessibility in terms of physical things like ramps and elevators. But sometimes there's this assumption that if you're a wheelchair user, you're a natural advocate, and we are not all advocates. If I could change one thing, it would be the narrative, people looking at us like we're a charity – and that's why Rollettes is not a non-profit any longer, we're a business.

Sometimes when people say they are inspired by me, I'm just living my life. If I'm at the grocery store and I'm reaching for something, or I'm out for dinner, that's not inspirational. But if someone came up to me at dance class and said I was inspirational, that's different.

My core group of Rollettes, and the girls who come to *Rollettes Experience*, certainly inspire me, and they give me the reason to do more. My friend Ali Stroker, who was the first person in a wheelchair to appear on Broadway, and has won a Tony Award, told me to turn your limitations into opportunities. That has stuck in my head. It really helps.

Chelsie's object
Hidden away in my closet, I have the last pair of jeans I ever wore. I lost all my muscle, so they don't fit me any longer. They represent the 17-year-old girl whose life was flipped upside down. In the beginning I was angry because they were my favourite pair of jeans – and then they motivated me to do physical therapy to build muscle back – and then I was more conscious of the great memories I have in those jeans. Now if I want to do physical therapy, I do it. But I don't feel I have to walk to accomplish anything.

HANNAH GRAF

There is something powerful about being your authentic self.

HANNAH GRAF

Hannah Graf came out as a transgender woman in 2013 and was one of the highest-ranking transgender soldiers in the British Army, serving with the Royal Electrical and Mechanical Engineers. A decorated officer, she became the Army's Transgender Representative and advised on transgender policy. In 2015, she was made a patron of Mermaids, one of the UK's leading LGBTQ+ charities. In 2019, she retired from the Army and was awarded an MBE.

I grew up in Cardiff with my mum, my dad, and older brother. As early as I can remember, I was questioning my gender. I'd never heard the word transgender; all I knew was that I didn't click with the body that I had or the role in society that people expected me to play. I spent a lot of my childhood and teenage years feeling unsettled and uneasy, and that I was the only person like me in the world.

I was in the Army Cadets and an instructor said, *'You could do this for a job.'* That piqued my interest and I applied to a military college where you did A Levels and military activities. Then I went to Newcastle University and got an engineering degree, before heading to the Royal Military Academy Sandhurst to become an officer.

There is a school of thought that, before we come out, transgender women choose hyper-masculine roles in order to prove to ourselves, and the wider world, that we are the men society says we are. That is partially true but, equally, I loved physical activity, being outdoors, the teamwork and camaraderie. I find it strange that people think that women – trans or otherwise – shouldn't be in the Army when there is nothing about those qualities that is inherently unfeminine.

Being a closeted trans person is a strange experience. On the outside I was happy: I'd been to Sandhurst, I'd become an officer and was in a leadership role. Everything seemed positive but I was living this hidden life. Everything came to a head on a tour of duty in Afghanistan. It's a place where there is no time off, you are working seven days a week and have no private space. I lived in a tent with seven guys and there was no internet access, no TV. It led to a large amount of introspection and I realised that, if I didn't do something, I was going to live an unhappy and unfulfilled life.

I didn't click with the body that I had or the role in society that people expected me to play.

The first steps were small. I went to the doctor and said, *'I think I might be trans, but I don't want it written down.'* The doctor said, *'We can't really treat you without putting it in medical notes.'* Eventually, I was talking to a military psychiatrist about how I was feeling, and they offered to connect me with a trans woman in the RAF. We started this email conversation, had calls and then met. To this day she is a good friend, and a transformative person in my life.

Coming out as trans is very long process and there are many different facets. There are physical changes, so that might be hormones and surgeries, but they are probably least important. What is really important is exploring your personality, who you are truly meant to be and your place in society.

In the armed forces we train to fight for our lives, and we are good at recognising people for what they can do rather than who they are. If you are fighting for your life, you are not going to care if the person next to you is female, trans, gay, bi, Muslim, Christian. What matters is – can you shoot straight? Can you run fast? And, if needs be, can you carry me home to my family? So, after I came out, I was fortunate that the people around me respected me and I just got on with being a good officer.

I told my family a little later. I was scared of losing them, I was scared of them feeling shame and disappointment, and grieving the life they thought I was going to have. I did it at Christmas and just said, *'I'm transgender.'* There were tears and shock and no one knew what to say or do, but they never let me feel that I wasn't loved and supported.

I knew way before my transition that it was the right thing. The only reason I hadn't come out sooner was fear of losing the respect of those I love, and being mocked and abused by society. When I didn't lose the respect of my colleagues or the love of my parents, or my friendships, I knew it was going to be okay and it became a journey of positivity and, with every step, I became happier.

I don't think my teenage self would believe where I am today. My husband is transgender and although that's what brought us together, it's not what keeps us together. He is the most brilliant filmmaker, husband and father. We had our child through surrogacy. A woman called Laura, who is an angel to us, recognised that we were just a couple who wanted a family and couldn't do it the natural way. In April 2020, she delivered our beautiful baby girl, Millie.

Everything seemed positive but I was living this hidden life.

When I decided to transition, I thought that I would be alone for the rest of my life because society had taught me that trans women were unlovable. I thought that was a sacrifice I had to make, so the idea that I am now married and have a child is just incredible. To any young person who is thinking about their gender and

whether it is aligned to what society thinks of them, I would say there is only one person that knows and that's you. There is something powerful about being your authentic self and, for the most part, people will love you for it.

I would love to see the media change the way it talks about trans people; it can be so damaging and misleading. We are just people who want to live happy, productive lives, the same as anyone else. I'd like to see feminism become as inclusive as it can be. A lot of people in the feminist community are very supportive of trans people but there are many who aren't. I see the fight against transphobia as a fight against misogyny and absolutely in line with feminist values. Let's support each other and try to do what's right for all women.

Hannah's object
My object is my sword, it was given to me by my parents as a passing out gift when I finished my year at Sandhurst. It symbolises my journey to become an officer. When I was given the sword, it was engraved with my name and the date that I passed out. When I transitioned, my dad said, *'Let's get the other side engraved with your new name and the date you transitioned.'* So, as well as a symbol of the values of leadership that I learned at Sandhurst, the sword became a symbol of the support of my parents, through thick and thin.

SHERYL CROW

Photography by Dove Shore

That was a real epiphany moment. My work was now solely mine. It was my vision. It was produced by me. It was engineered by a woman.

SHERYL CROW

Sheryl Crow began her career by recording jingles for advertising clients, before becoming a backup singer for stars like Michael Jackson and Rod Stewart. She hit the big time with her 1993 debut album *Tuesday Night Music Club*, and continued to rack up accolades and massive sales with follow-up efforts like *Sheryl Crow and The Globe Sessions*. With nine Grammy Awards under her belt, Crow announced that her 2019 album, *Threads*, would be her last. Her albums have garnered nine Grammys and sold over 50 million units worldwide.

I grew up in a very small town in the Southern bootheel of Missouri. It was a church-oriented, close-knit community. I had a pretty idyllic upbringing where everyone knew everyone and all the parents looked out for all the kids.

My mom and dad were very musical. My mom was a piano teacher and all four of us kids took piano lessons. At a pretty young age I realised I could play by ear. It was entertaining to adults, and I kind of formulated my persona around that.

When I was in school, I played in cover bands, which was a fantastic training ground. Then I went to Saint Louis University and took a teaching degree. I immediately got into a band and played in more cover bands. After a couple years of doing that, I got some session work in a studio to sing a McDonald's commercial. That commercial was picked up nationwide and it made me more money in 45 minutes of work than I had made from two years of teaching. So I decided to move to LA with the money I made to see if I could get my songs heard. And that was the beginning of my journey.

I drove around with a big book of maps and took my tapes to every recording studio in LA. I wound up getting some background work. I overheard some singers talking about an audition for Michael Jackson, and I toured with him as a backing vocalist during his *Bad* tour in the 80s.

It wasn't until I came home from the Jackson tour that I realised everybody who held all the cards in LA were men. There was one female who embraced me from a publishing company. Her name was Judy Stakee, and she was a huge champion for me. She helped me not only in learning how to write better songs, but in setting me up with other songwriters. But other than that, it was all male. It really took a long time to embrace my own power.

I sold nine million copies of my first record, then when my male producer left, I decided to produce my second record myself. My manager said, *'Do you know what you're doing?'* And I had to fight for it. That was a real epiphany moment. My work was now solely mine. It was my vision. It was produced by me. It was engineered by a woman. But it also opened the doors for other young women to say, *'If she produced her record and it was successful, then why can't I do the same?'* And because that record became so successful, it gave me permission to continue to produce myself. That was what navigated the future for me.

Once I got sick with breast cancer, I had to examine my self appointed role of being a caretaker and a people pleaser. That for me was a real turning point in learning how to put myself first and learning to say no, at the risk of people not being happy with me. It was very liberating. Two of the most beautiful things that came out of it were me adopting my two boys.

Although I came into motherhood as an older mom, by the time my boys came, I had done everything I wanted to. The gift for me was being able to say, *'There is nothing else that I would rather be doing.'* There's something really beautiful about having all of your attention go to the very thing that brings you the most joy.

As a teenager, I could never have envisioned that I would have had the life that I've had. But I wish I could go back and tell myself to have more fun. I'm always telling my boys to stop, look around and take in this moment, because life goes by so fast.

As a teenager, I could never have envisioned that I would have had the life that I've had. But I wish I could go back and tell myself to have more fun.

I look at women today, and I wouldn't want to be coming out as an artist now. Too much of it is weighted on your persona, your brand, your looks and your perfection. I can't imagine what that does to someone's self-esteem, especially as you age.

I worry that this younger generation perceives feminism as being able to wield their sexual beauty. I worry what it will mean as they grapple with ageing. Unless you really have the strength and the fortitude to allow yourself to age, it can be devastating to have society decide what roles you should be playing, and what clothes you should be wearing. As women we suffer being disqualified as we get old. But ageing is something to be honoured and celebrated, as opposed to being fixed. You have to embrace and own the beautiful aspects of getting older and wiser.

The idea of everyone having an equal footing would be wonderful: that we're all standing on the same level ground with it being about the quality of what we can bring as opposed to our looks; that it's about our hard work and our voice; and that it's not unusual for a woman to have a high position and equal pay. We've come so far, and yet we have so far to go. We have to rewrite our roles. It's uncomfortable and it's sometimes unpleasant, but it's also euphoric and celebratory.

Sheryl's object
My significant object is this Gibson Country and Western guitar which I bought 35 years ago. I refer to as *'The Little Moneymaker'* because almost anything I made money off of, I wrote on that guitar. I bought it in 1991 at a guitar shop in Los Angeles. When I played it, I knew it was coming home with me. It's my go-to guitar. I feel like it's had many lives. When you play a guitar, you leave some of that life experience on its neck and on its body. It's a tried and true friend. It's been there to support and help me find myself and my voice. It's a beauty.

KATARINA JOHNSON-THOMPSON

*I used to define my self-worth
by my achievements on the track.
But you have to separate your
work from your personal life and
separate your expectations from
other people's expectations.*

KATARINA JOHNSON-THOMPSON

Heptathlete Katarina Johnson-Thompson is the current World Number 1 ranked Heptathlete and won the gold medal at the 2018 Commonwealth Games and the 2019 World Championships, breaking the British record with a score of 6,981 points. She also holds the British record of 5,000 points for the Women's Pentathlon, winning gold at the 2015 and 2019 European Indoor Championships, as well as in the 2018 World Indoor Championships. She was the 2012 World Junior Long Jump champion and holds the British High Jump record with 1.98 m outdoors (2016) and 1.97 m indoors (2015). Johnson-Thompson's heptathlon results include finishing 14th at the 2012 London Olympics, fifth at the 2013 World Championships, sixth at the 2016 Rio Olympics and second at the 2018 European Championships. She currently lives in Montpellier, France.

I was born in Liverpool. For the first year of my life, I lived in Nassau in the Bahamas, where my dad came from. After my mum and I came back to the cold north of England, my first house was a pub, which my nan and grandad ran. Although I am an only child, I grew up with a lot of family around me, a lot of cousins.

My mum was a can-can dancer. She travelled the world, which is how she met my dad in the Bahamas. She really wanted that life for me. When I was first walking, just out of nappies, she had me doing ballet dancing, modern and classical tap. I was super-sporty, always playing football, running around, the total opposite of a dancer, and when I gave up ballet she was very upset. She said I had to have a hobby, so we tried football and keyboard lessons and finally athletics – which she didn't like at first, though now she loves it so much that she says she wishes she could have done it herself. I think in my lifetime she's only missed three of my competitions. She's always been there, supporting me – especially when I lost, believing in me.

I didn't know what I wanted to do other than athletics when I was a kid and I still don't know what I want to do other than athletics. I've always wanted to win an Olympic medal, and I still haven't done it – yet. I wasn't the best student at school because I always wanted to be on the track. But I've still got friends from school to this day, and they are my core group of friends.

I was the tallest in my class at primary school and they put me in for the high jump. I am a heptathlete now – I do seven different events – but high jump is where it all started. In Year 6 I did a 1.32m scissor kick, which was a record at the time. When you break a record, you realise no one's ever done it before. It's not simply the best of the kids who were around at the time, it's the best ever. It was then I thought that maybe I should join a club.

When I was 19, I competed in the London 2012 Olympics. That was a huge moment for me: I realised that this was what it was all about, the pinnacle. As a heptathlete it's hard to be consistent enough across all the events to qualify. Once I was at that level, in the years from 2012 to 2016, it was a big learning curve. I failed a lot; I progressed a lot – and then the years from 2016 until now are when I'm reaping the rewards.

As a teenager, going through puberty and going out to compete in a crop-top and knickers, I would worry more about what I looked like than about my performance.

In athletics, we think in Olympic cycles. In 2012, I was young to be competing, buzzing to be part of the competition. In 2016 (the Rio Olympics) I was still young, 23, but I put a lot of weight on my shoulders to come out with a medal, thinking that this is what people expect, this is what I expect. And I just wasn't ready, physically or mentally. I wasn't in the right place at the time. Now, when I look to the 2020/2021 Olympics, I feel ready.

After the disappointment of 2016, I changed my life. I sold my house, I moved to France. I changed coach; it was a complete reset.

Athletics requires you to put your whole self out there for judgement. You're saying, *'this is my best self and what I've worked for, and this is my performance.'* As a teenager, going through puberty and going out to compete in a crop-top and knickers, I would worry more about what I looked like than about my performance. In 2012, there were 80,000 people in the stadium and millions watching through the lens of a camera. Once I'd experienced that, I thought nothing else was going to be as terrifying.

The great thing about athletics is that you can see progress. I love the way that when you start a season you do a session of training and then, three weeks later, you're able to complete it, where you weren't at first. I like pushing myself. But I sometimes haven't coped well with losing. After a loss on a major stage, I'd wake up and it would be the first thing I'd think about. And you can't beat yourself up like that – we're all just trying our best. Being kind to yourself sets you up for a better life and a better performance because the *'what ifs'* don't matter.

I still want to win Olympic gold. That's the ultimate achievement. People in athletics can sometimes pin gold on you before you've got the ability to achieve it and I think that happened to me. I doubted I could achieve Olympic gold when other people thought I

could – and that's a lot to deal with when you're young. I didn't cope very well, and that shows in my results from 2014 to 2016.

When my performances were really bad, I'd see myself as a failure. A lot of people would believe in me, and I'd think, *'Why are people putting these dreams on me when I don't belong here at the track? I'm clearly not a heptathlete. My body can't handle heptathlon because I get injured. I can't handle the pressure on a big stage because I keep flopping. Why are they expecting me to do well?'*

I used to define my self-worth by my achievements on the track. But you have to separate your work from your personal life and separate your expectations from other people's expectations. Now, when I go into an event, I know what it's taken me to get there. It's all about self-belief and focusing on what you need to do.

Katarina's object

My Liverpool Harriers club vest is the first vest I wore, apart from at primary school. From there I wore a county vest and then eventually I was competing at the Olympics in a Team GB vest. I owe my whole life to sport, and the Liverpool Harriers is where it all started.

VANESSA XUEREB

Vanessa Xuereb is the Chief Membership Officer at Soho House Group and widely regarded as one of the most important women in hospitality. With a career that spans over 24 years at the members' club, she is one of the original founding team members recruited by CEO and Founder Nick Jones. She works closely with Jones; he sets the vision while she is the ultimate host, owning *'front of house'* and completely focused on members, guests and key events. Vanessa is passionate about the business and is responsible for Soho House's diverse membership across 30 Houses globally.

I grew up in Brixton and have lived there all my life. My family is loving and crazy. At school I was quite curious, but I don't fully remember my youth because, at the age of 21, I suffered a head injury after being hit by a car. I lost all of my memory. After the injury, I had to relearn everything; people's names, where I met them, what had happened. I even forgot how to drive. The head injury changed my life, I couldn't walk for about three months and had a whole host of problems. I was really unwell for about two years and had very bad PTSD. I also had a stutter and lost all of my confidence. I relied on my friends and family to tell me what had happened. After the accident, it made me value every moment even more – because my life changed in a split second and I'm just very lucky that I came out of it.

I was going to be an actress. I was studying and about to go to drama school but the accident took that future away from me. A friend who was living with me at the time started working at Soho House and she asked me to cover her shift on reception one day. I did and I've never left. Starting at Soho House made me more independent and I gained so much confidence. Now Soho House is my home.

From receptionist I became Reception Manager, then Members' Relations Manager, then Member Relations Director and then last year I was given the new role of Chief Membership Officer across the world. I remember so well what it felt like being the receptionist and looking up and seeing and hearing about the c-suite and the leaders and it meant so much that I was considered to be part of that team. I've made it. By staying and investing my talents in the business I was rewarded with trust and promotion – and a job I absolutely love doing. Every day is different and stimulating. I feel fulfilled and happy, and that comes from feeling respected, needed and valued. I think what I love most about my work is that I love people; the interaction, the connections, and finding out what's happening in their lives.

There is a sense of *'family'* that the Soho House team expresses – that sense that everyone is valued and welcomed. This feeling is what has made them a huge success and they have grown and expanded because of it. The key to success is: work hard and be kind to people.

If I could give my teenage self some advice I would tell her to stop worrying about what other people think. Stop pleasing other people, just think about what makes you happy.

Vanessa's object
My object is a photo of my mum, my dad and my brother in a gold heart frame. I've travelled a lot for work and this picture is something that I always take with me and put by my bedside. I'm really homey and quite rooted. I love being able to travel but this brings me home to my family. It's the strength and love that my family gave me that has given me the confidence to be who I am.

LUCY EDWARDS

I believe that knowledge is power, and when you equip someone with knowledge about people, then that group of people is more accepted in society.

LUCY EDWARDS

Lucy Edwards is a blind broadcaster and disability activist. She trained as a BBC journalist and was the first blind presenter on BBC Radio 1. Her YouTube and TikTok posts show her experiences of blindness; she also collaborated with Guide Dogs on the *Blind Hacks* YouTube series. She works with various charities in the sight-loss sector, and she has toured schools to promote the Fixers UK charity, which champions the potential of young people, after collaborating in the writing of *The Superhero Dog*, a children's book about her guide dog, Olga. She is also the author of *The Blind Beauty Guide*. In 2017 she received the *Guide Dogs Young Persons Achievements Award* for her contributions to the sight-loss community.

I grew up in Birmingham in the West Midlands. I had a really lovely childhood. I've got a sister who's only 15 months younger than me – when we were younger, we looked like twins. I adore her. I had a lovely group of friends at school – I'm still friends with them to this day. My two best friends, Beth and Connie, have been by my side for ever.

You can be independent and live a full and amazing life without sight.

At 17 years old, in the middle of my A-levels, I went completely blind, pretty much overnight, because of my eyesight condition, incontinentia pigmenti, which I've had since I was 11. When I lost my vision, I had to learn to walk, talk, eat again. The rehabilitation process took years. I felt so low. Having my main sense ripped away from me, I would just sit there. I did know cane skills, but I didn't really embrace them because I didn't want to be blind. My whole being, every atom in me, was trying to repel this massive thing that was happening. I was traumatised. I had all these lovely, loving people around me – my sister, my mum, my dad, my boyfriend – all saying, *'Look, it's going to be OK,'* but not really knowing what to do. I was sick with grief so many mornings. I woke up and the reality would hit me: you can't see. For about a year and a half, I couldn't be alone for long. I was always with my mum; I was always talking on my phone if I wasn't with anyone, because it was so scary to be in the dark. I was on strong medication because I was so low and depressed.

Then I started to believe in the social model of disability. That's when the rest of the world outside needs to change and adapt to me, rather than the medical model that says, *'Lucy, you need fixing.'* For so long, my mindset was the medical model, and it was really detrimental to my health. I was thinking, *'I hope for a cure one day,'* or *'I hope that I regain my vision, and I wish that this never happened.'* It was so toxic to my thought processes. When I switched, that is when my life changed.

My ambition as a young girl was to follow an advocacy path and I dreamed of standing up for the rights of disabled people. I trained for a term at law school, but I found that social media and journalism and storytelling were more me – telling my story because I had overcome so much. I just couldn't stop shouting from the rooftops about how you can be independent and live a full and amazing life without sight. There was not a lot of information about blindness – I didn't see myself represented in the media.

I started to look at media jobs and I saw *Extend in Digital News* on the BBC website – a scheme to get disabled journalists into the industry. I got training, I met some of my best friends on the whole entire planet, and I just was really overwhelmed with telling other people's stories. I learned so much about myself.

When the pandemic hit, I guess everyone just pressed pause on their life. I was thinking, *'What is this TikTok thing?'* My sister was scrolling with me one day, and she said, *'Lu, this is really cool.'* Also my sister-in-law was massive on the dances and tried to move my arms in the positions for all of them. *#LearnOnTikTok* is my thing! I started to think about it in a journalistic way, because a strapline was needed to get my message across. And *#HowDoesABlindGirl* was born. People in my life who don't live with me – Connie, Beth, all of my school friends – and don't see me interact with the world on a day-to-day basis knew lots about how I navigate, but didn't necessarily know how I do really basic things. They were really interested, and then everyone else was too, it was kind of a ripple effect. I uploaded my day-to-day of how I pour a drink, how I go about my daily life, how I read documents, and in less than a year, I got 1.5 million followers.

I set out to make sure that people are more educated on blindness.

With my videos, I set out to make sure that people are more educated on blindness, because I know that there's loads of people who have so many questions that maybe they're embarrassed to ask, or they aren't sure if it's appropriate. Maybe you've never interacted with a blind person, you've only seen them on TV shows or passing by in your school or workplace, and you want to know how they live their life. I want it to be common knowledge. I believe that knowledge is power, and when you equip someone with knowledge about people, then that group of people is more accepted in society.

So many things have led to this point in my life: a feeling of happiness and contentment. I felt for so long I had to prove something to myself; that I was running this race with my own mind over what I used to be, and

comparing what I used to be able to see and what I used to be able to do. So much of me just longed so badly for yesterday, rather than being happy with tomorrow. Comparing myself to past me was so toxic – like everyone looking at social media and comparing themselves to other people. I'm glad now I can't see Instagram or social media. I believe it's one of my blessings.

I think the best advice I've even been given was from my late grandpa, my mum's dad: don't worry about something until it's happened. There have been so many times when I've felt so anxious about an event, or a time in my life, but actually, when I got there, it was fine. So: thank you, Grandpa.

Lucy's object
I have a mirror, which sounds weird because I can't see in it. It's a little heart-shaped compact. Alice, my sister, gave it to me when I could see, it makes me so emotional. I think back to all that we've been through and all the struggles we've had, and all the depression and anxiety. We've always been a constant. The mirror is a symbol of her being my mirror – and her never letting me ever not feel good about myself.

TAKE YOURSELF OUT
OF YOUR
COMFORT ZONE.
THOSE ARE THE
MOMENTS WHERE YOU
LEARN
THE MOST AND
FEEL A REAL
SENSE OF
ACHIEVEMENT.

NICOLA MENDELSOHN

WORK

Locating the barriers to ambition and fulfilment.

The landscape for women at work has changed significantly over the last century but has not yet reached parity. Bias against women exists in many workplace policies and practices, because they were originally designed by men, for men.

The Female Lead published a study in 2021, led by Dr Terri Apter, exploring the barriers women face at work. The study found many outdated myths, which block positive change in workplaces. For example, the presumptions that 'motherhood shifts a woman's professional identity to the backseat', or that 'female workers are more averse to embracing new challenges and risks.' These myths, and many more, are damaging to women's progression and part of The Female Lead's mission is to amplify the voices of women whose stories bust those myths.

It is clear from the women profiled in this book that they care passionately about creating change; change that helps women manage the many roles they must blend at home and at work. Dismantling some of the outdated structures created by men, for men, is vital. But bringing men along in this quest is essential. For men too will benefit from working conditions that better reflect the changed world that we live in, and because true equality at work will stimulate economic growth for everyone.

No country can ever truly flourish if it stifles the potential of its women and deprives itself of the contributions of half of its citizens.
MICHELLE OBAMA

LADY BRENDA HALE

In this day and age, it is no longer legitimate for a small group of upper-middle-class, privately educated white men to be laying down the law for the rest of society.

LADY BRENDA HALE

Brenda Hale was President of the Supreme Court from 2017 to 2020, when she retired at the age of 75. In 1984, she was the first woman to be appointed to the Law Commission and her work was key to the introduction of the Children Act 1989, the Family Law Act 1996 and the Mental Capacity Act 2005. She became a High Court Judge in 1994. In 1999 she was the second woman to be promoted to the Court of Appeal, before becoming the first female Law Lord in 2004. She was made a life peer, taking the title Baroness Hale of Richmond. Her most famous ruling as President of the Supreme Court was in September 2019, when she declared Prime Minister Boris Johnson's suspension of Parliament unlawful. She became a household name, her spider brooch was celebrated on T-shirts, and her journey from Yorkshire schoolgirl to head of the UK's highest court is the subject of a children's book and her forthcoming memoir, *Spider Woman*.

I grew up in a village called Scorton, five miles from the town of Richmond in north Yorkshire. My father was headmaster of a small independent boys' boarding school; my mother ran the boarding house and also did some teaching.

I am the middle of three sisters. We went to the girls' high school in Richmond and all three of us became head girl in due course. Our parents were pleased that we passed the 11 plus exam, but that was expected. What was also expected was that we would go to university if we could. I was the first from my school both to go to Cambridge and to study law.

There is so much to like about the law – it is an amazingly varied subject and affects every area of our lives.

In the sixties, very few girls were studying law and even fewer were practising. I thought about becoming a barrister but was advised that this was not a suitable career for a woman with no connections. I thought about becoming a solicitor but that involved more exams almost straight away, and I'd worked so hard at Cambridge I didn't fancy that. So I went to teach law at the University of Manchester, choosing Manchester because they wanted me to qualify as a barrister in my spare time and

practise alongside teaching. It seemed the best of both worlds.

I never thought of becoming a judge – there were hardly any woman judges then – but everything I did as a university lecturer led, one way or the other, to a public appointment. For example, I wrote a book about mental health law and that led to my first judicial appointment as a presiding member on mental health review tribunals, deciding whether people should stay confined in psychiatric hospitals.

I went on to become a Law Commissioner promoting the reform of the law. Around the same time, the Lord Chancellor's department wanted to diversify the judiciary – not by having more women, but by having academics with practitioner experience as part-time judges. I spent nine years being a Law Commissioner and a part-time judge and that led, eventually, to the High Court bench which led to the Court of Appeal, and then to the top court in the country which was the Appellate Committee of the House of Lords. Then, in 2009, the House of Lords Committee became the Supreme Court of the United Kingdom.

I defy anybody not to have had imposter syndrome and be any good at what they do. When I first went to the high school, the only girl from my little village school, I thought,

'What I am doing here?' When I went to Cambridge, I pinched myself and thought, *'I am so pleased to be here, but is it me?'* When I went to the Law Commission – the first woman, and surrounded by very confident, intellectually impressive people – I thought, *'Can I really do it?'*

The best advice that I have been given was – do it. When I was a full-time academic and it was suggested that I became a part-time judge, that was strange and scary. I asked the opinion of four professors at the University of Manchester: two said it would be a distraction from my academic career so I had better not; the other two said, do it. And if I hadn't, I would not have had the life that I have.

The best advice that I have been given was – do it.

On my coat of arms is the motto *omnia feminae aequissimae*, which means that women are equal to everything. I wanted to make a statement of my belief that women are the equals of men and should have equal rights and responsibilities. In this day and age, it is no longer legitimate for a small group of upper-middle-class, privately educated white men to be laying down the law for the rest of society.

Women make up half the human race but other diversity in the judiciary is also important. Ethnic, socio-economic diversity, sexual orientation – there are all sorts of ways in which people are different from one another. The courts are there to serve the public as a whole and they ought to be seen by the public as diverse, and therefore legitimate in exercising authority. The law is there to uphold the values of justice, fairness and equality and if the judiciary don't visibly embody all three, then they are not reflecting what the law is about.

There is so much to like about the law – it is an amazingly varied subject and affects every area of our lives, it isn't just about punishing criminals. I am proud of some of the legislation which my team at the Law Commission promoted and was successful in changing the law for the better. I am proud of some of the judgments which I made at all levels in the courts – not just the House of Lords or the Supreme Court; and the judgment of the Supreme Court in the prorogation case against the Prime Minister is a source of quiet satisfaction.

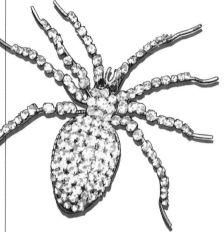

Lady Hale's object
My spider brooch sums up my life and career. I was wearing it when I went into the principal courtroom in the Supreme Court to deliver the summary of the judgment in the prorogation case. I had carefully chosen the dress that I was going to wear, a demure black number. I have a lot of brooches – my dear late husband gave them to me to cheer up the sober garments that I was expected to wear as a high court judge. The brooches tend to migrate to particular garments and stay there, and with that dress was the spider. I didn't give it a second thought. It was only after the event that I realised that that brooch had captured the imagination of millions of people worldwide, who were wondering whether it contained a message. I didn't know that The Who had a song called *Boris the Spider* until somebody sent me a YouTube recording, and I regret to say that *Boris the Spider* comes to a sticky end. Had I known, I might have chosen a different brooch.

*Find a community, find a tribe,
find people to learn things with.*

ANNE-MARIE IMAFIDON

Anne-Marie Imafidon was the youngest girl ever to pass A-level computing. She has worked at companies such as Goldman Sachs, Hewlett-Packard and Deutsche Bank. She holds honorary doctorates from the Open University, Glasgow Caledonian University, Kent University and Bristol University, and an honorary fellowship at Keble College, Oxford. A visiting professor at the University of Sunderland, she sits on the Council of Research England. She was appointed MBE in 2017 for services to young women and STEM (science, technology, engineering and mathematics) sectors. Anne-Marie is the CEO and Co-Founder of Stemettes, which was launched in 2013. She is also a Trustee at the Institute of Work and was named most influential woman in UK IT in 2020.

I grew up across east London, which is the best place on Earth. We lived in Stratford, South Woodford, Canning Town – all *E* postcodes. My family is large – I'm one of five children – and we laugh a lot and enjoy ourselves. My family is British Nigerian, so there's everything that comes with that, whether it's the jollof rice, being in church a lot, or placing a lot of value on education.

Technology is so deep-seated, so deep-rooted, it's part of everything we do.

My parents were very laid-back and relaxed. They were open to us trying all kinds of different things. Their thing was: *'If you're going to do it, do it well. We're not going to say no and get in your way. We're going to do what we can to allow you to flourish as much as you can, and see where this goes.'* I did two GCSEs aged 10: one in maths and one in ICT. Aged 11, I did my computing A Level, and I did an AS in maths, and I went up to study at Oxford aged 17. I'd finished my master's by the time I was 20.

In terms of being underestimated, this is something I'm encountering much more as an adult than I did as a child. I'm always the youngest, the blackest, the female-est person, whether it's in board meetings, in pitch scenarios, in media, in certain rooms. For me it's always a funny one, almost, to kind of play the underdog, and arrive at the event and be treated a particular way – and then watch the shock on the faces when I stand up, and I am the keynote, part of the reason why they turned up.

Stemettes is a social enterprise that I run. We're engaging, we're inspiring, we're supporting girls and non-binary young people aged from five up to 25. We run longer-term intersectional cohort programmes; mid-length, mid-term impactful events; and a couple of inspirational content platforms. We aim to show that girls do STEM – STEM is for all, and that there's a lot of opportunity and fulfilment in this. And there are a lot of reasons why this is definitely something you can do, despite what the world might be telling you.

My favourite part of my work is sitting with young people and seeing them discover something for the first time.

Stemettes started in 2013 because I noticed that the lack of women in technical fields was a serious problem. Technology is so deep-seated, so deep-rooted, it's part of everything we do: the way we communicate, the way we transact, the way we understand things. Not having women there means that you're rebuilding a second-class citizen based on gender, and that's not good enough. We deserve better for what happens next. We deserve our own agency, our own understanding of the world around us, and the world deserves to have our perspective and our experience baked into what they're consuming and the technology they're using – the technology that's making decisions about their lives.

What I love about my work are the eureka moments and the positivity in the community of *Stemettes* that we've built, created and nurtured. My favourite thing about my job is not the photo shoots, the TV appearances, the books that I'm writing, the time on stage, the board meetings or any of that.

My favourite part of my work is sitting with young people and seeing them discover something for the first time, seeing their eyes opened to possibilities, helping them unlearn the conditioning they will have inevitably got from their parents, from peers, from teachers, from the TV, from media, on this whole thing about technical women being an impossibility or not even existing.

For me, the joy is the connections they make. We've got something called the Stemette Society, and they're global and they're on it all day, talking to each other, helping each other, solving problems, and it's so nice to just go on there and see the connections being made, the problems being solved, see people celebrating each other.

If my teenage self could see me now, she would think, *'OK, wow! This is where we got to! This is how it ended up; I see!'* The advice I would give my teenage self is the advice I give myself now: Anne-Marie, you should take yourself more seriously! I really don't, and I really should. I'm always game for a laugh

and I'm always wanting to enjoy myself, whatever situation I'm in. So I wish, as a teenager, I could have learned to sit still and take things seriously, just a little bit.

To other teenagers, I would say: don't do things alone. You can spend a lot of time trying to learn and discover things on your own, to explore on your own, whereas having folks to do that with means that you will probably stick at it longer, you'll have an enriched learning experience. And it's nicer to do things with other people. Find a community, find a tribe, find people to learn things with. You'll have people to answer your questions – and people to celebrate your wins with you.

Anne-Marie's object
I chose my BlackBerry from around 2006, 2007. I have a lot of good memories with my BlackBerry. It sent a message: this is someone who's going somewhere; this is someone who's super-busy, has a finger in a lot of pies, and needs all of them on a device that's always with her. Picking it up, all the memories came back. I don't know if I'm sentimentally attached to the BlackBerry itself, or the time of my life I had that BlackBerry for.

JOY CROOKES

A proud South Londoner of Bangladeshi and Irish heritage, Joy Crookes is a multi-hyphenate artist shaped by a rich tapestry of influences. She's a singer–songwriter and multi instrumentalist. In 2020, Joy made the prestigious BRITS *Rising Star Award* shortlist, as well as placing fourth on the BBC *Sound Poll*, and headlining *'ones to watch'* lists from YouTube Music, Amazon Music, MTV Push, NME and beyond. Renowned for her live performances, Joy has played Glastonbury, BBC Radio 1's *Big Weekend* and *Later...With Jools Holland*, as well as selling out her own headline tours across the UK and Europe.

I grew up in south London, in Elephant and Castle. My family are Bangladeshi Irish: my dad was born and raised in Ireland, my mum born and raised in Bangladesh.

At school I was good at studying and my ambition was to do really well. I've always been competitive and have a strong work ethic. I also tried to have as much fun as possible and I was a bit of a chatterbox and a class clown.

There was always music in my house. I loved music, I felt that it could say everything that I couldn't. Music is my voice, it's the only way that I can get absolutely everything out. As much as I am quite an honest person, sometimes my music speaks before my talking voice.

The advice I would give to someone who wants to become a musician or artist is to write your own songs. When you focus on your craft or an instrument and you hone that skill, there is less room for doubt. It gives you confidence and clarity in what you want to become. I am not the most talented piano or guitar player but I used those skills as tools to further my songwriting.

Society doesn't naturally favour women and my experience in the music industry is that I have sometimes had to be loud for people to hear my voice. And that takes confidence, and self-assurance and self-belief to make that noise and be heard.

To get to the point where I am now, it's been a lot of hard work. I wish that young people knew that to become an artist – whether that be a musician, a painter or a filmmaker – takes time.

Impostor syndrome is inevitable for anyone who works with the public. I don't ignore it, I acknowledge it: okay, you're there, but I still need to write these songs and get on this stage. I think that learning to live with the voice in my head has actually made it quieter.

Joy's object
We learned about Frida Kahlo in GCSE Art. Seeing her embrace her Mexican side even though she was half German made me think about my Bangladeshi side. I asked my mum if we could go to Alperton in north-west London to buy some pretty things. I was connecting to something within myself. I bought ten pairs of traditional earrings called jhumkas. The earrings were my entry point to connecting with my heritage, but also being proud of it. Without my earrings, I wouldn't be at the point I am now with my identity.

SHAZIA MIRZA

I want it to be normal that when a woman comes on stage and is funny, people don't have to point out that she's a woman.

SHAZIA MIRZA

Shazia Mirza is a comedian, actor and writer. She was the first Muslim woman on the UK comedy circuit. Born in Birmingham, she studied biochemistry at the University of Manchester and taught science in a London school while studying acting and comedy at the same time. She has written a column in The Guardian, and The New Statesman and writes for other newspapers and magazines; she has appeared on television, including on *Have I Got News For You*; and in shows *Celebrity Island with Bear Grylls* on Channel 4, *Celebs in Solitary*, and *Celebrity Supply Teacher* for the BBC. Her standup comedy show *The Kardashians Made Me Do It*, a satire on political correctness, premiered at the Tricycle Theatre, had seven sell-out runs at London's Soho Theatre, and toured Europe and the USA.

My parents were very traditional, very conservative. They originally came from Pakistan and moved to England in the sixties. Their hope for me was that I would be well-educated and successful. It was a strict Muslim household: I had to adhere to rules and regulations. I have three brothers and one sister, and they wanted all their children to be doctors.

The fact that I'm not a doctor is a tragedy to them. I haven't even played a doctor in *Crossroads* or *Holby City*. They feel really disappointed. The only option for me was to be a doctor – or if I did badly, maybe a dentist or a lawyer. My job as a comedian is never discussed.

> *The only option for me was to be a doctor – or if I did badly, maybe a dentist or a lawyer. My job as a comedian is never discussed.*

My parents have never come to see me perform. They watch me on television, but they never comment. When I go home we sit around the dinner table and they talk about Donald Trump, the Kardashians, and anything else that's in the news. But they never mention what I do. I think they feel that if they talked about it, they would somehow have endorsed it.

Even when people stop my parents in the street in Birmingham and say: *'I saw your daughter on TV,'* my dad will answer: *'Well, you know, she has a degree in biochemistry. She's a scientist, really.'* Sometimes if I'm on tour, I'll do a gig and then drive back down the motorway to stay with them. They won't ever ask how it went.

This is how it's always been. I'm used to it. I think there was a point where they thought I might give up and we wouldn't need to talk about it, but I never gave up and it's never been talked about.

I was very naughty at school. I was an attention seeker. I used to ask the teacher if I could go to the toilet in the middle of lessons and then I'd hide all the other children's coats so they couldn't find them at playtime. One of the first times I was on stage, I played Mary Magdalene in the school play. It was a serious scene: I had to find the body in the tomb. Everybody started laughing when I came on stage. I got told off. But I loved generating laughter.

We used to watch a lot of comedy on TV at home. The comedians were always white men so I didn't think that was something I could do. I tried to comply. My parents said: *'You can only go to university if you do something scientific.'* I didn't want to spend seven years training to be a doctor, so I decided to do a degree in biochemistry, which is not what I wanted to do; I wanted to do drama. And then I became a science teacher in a school in the East End of London. I was 21 years old. I was mainly teaching 16-year-old boys. I didn't want to be there and neither did they.

To keep 30 boys interested in science when I wasn't really interested in science myself, I had to be entertaining. After a while, I realised I was doing standup. I was getting up in the morning and just trying to be funny. They never thought I was funny. The worst heckles I ever got were from those kids. Nobody has ever stood up at one of my gigs and said: *'Oh God, when is this going to end?'*

I had never been to a comedy club before I did standup. I didn't know that there were gigs or a circuit. I went to a comedy class and the teacher told us that we had to tell the truth about our lives. In the first class, she said: *'I want you to talk about something true that is painful or makes you angry.'* And I spoke about how I had a moustache. I had a lot of facial hair; I had a beard at the time. I wrote a routine about how I tried to get rid of it and I bleached it and looked like Father Christmas.

The teacher said I should go on the comedy circuit and do this routine. I'd never thought of it as funny, but I started performing and people laughed. So, when people ask where material comes from, it's your life. And no matter how awful it might be, you can always make it funny.

I was the first Muslim woman to do standup in this country and one of the first in the world. As a result, people put pressure on me to talk about suicide bombers, and terrorism, and why things were getting blown up. I said: *'I don't know all these people. We don't have one big WhatsApp group where everybody knows what everybody else is doing.'*

I didn't want to be a spokesperson, I just wanted to be a great comedian. That meant I had to tell the truth about my life. I struggled

with it because I didn't want people to be uncomfortable. It took a bit of time and confidence. My teenage self wouldn't believe I'd had the balls to do it. The advice I'd give her is believe in yourself. People told me that; they told me to keep going because, when you really want to give up, that's probably the point that you're going to break through. It turned out to be good advice.

There were very few women doing comedy when I started, and I'm really pleased that there are now more women and more diverse voices. I want it to be normal that when a woman comes on stage and is funny, people don't have to point out that she's a woman.

Shazia's object

My object is my tap dancing shoes. The first time I appeared on stage I was tap dancing in a school play. I couldn't tap dance, but I had the shoes and I really wanted to learn. I bought those shoes knowing that my parents would never let me go to tap dancing classes, because it wasn't allowed. Later, I did learn to tap dance – and I think sometimes you have to lie to yourself and make yourself believe you can do it. And then you will.

GABRIELLA DI LACCIO

*I wanted to blend in at
the beginning, I wanted to
become more English and
that was a mistake.*

GABRIELLA DI LACCIO

Gabriella Di Laccio is an award-winning soprano, recording artist, curator and activist, who has become one of the leading voices in the fight for gender equality in music worldwide. Gabriella was born in Brazil and followed her dreams to become an international classical singer with a career in opera, oratorio and chamber music. She was the winner of the *Air Europa Classical Act of the Year* award in 2013, and in 2018, she was listed as one of the BBC's 100 *Most Inspirational and Influential Women in the World*. Gabriella is also the founder and the passionate driving force behind the Donne Foundation, an internationally recognised charity that celebrates, advances and amplifies women in music.

I grew up in south Brazil, in a small town. My parents' focus was to give us a good education and they worked really hard for that. Also, they gave me one of the best gifts any child can have – the freedom to dream. I could dream without boundaries, without them asking, *'Are you sure?'* For me, this was a priceless gift.

When I was growing up, I imagined singing all over the world, but I also wanted to be an ice skater or a gymnast. I didn't know that being a classical singer could be a profession so, when I finished high school, my plan was to start a degree in architecture.

The first time I performed live as a soloist, I was 17 years old. It was the first time I had the feeling of being able to move people with music. For two and a half years, I did music on the side and then I gave up architecture and never looked back. I love what I do for a living. It doesn't matter if there are 1,000 people or five, if I can see that people are happy, I feel I've done my job well.

If I could give my teenage self some advice I would say, stop worrying about your weight and the way you look, and focus on discovering who you are inside. There is a quote by Picasso that I love: *'Every child is an artist, the problem is how to remain an artist once you grow up.'* That quote speaks to me and reminds me how privileged I am for having parents who never questioned my crazy dreams.

I have a project called Donne (donne means women in Italian). I started this project because I found out that there were more than 6,000 female composers in the history of classical music. I was shocked and then I was angry. I was angry because I grew up far away from Europe, from the world that I was dreaming of being part of and I heard stories of heroes, of geniuses who had to fight adversity like dyslexic Einstein or deaf Beethoven. When I found out that there were women in the history of music with stories too, I decided to start a project to promote women in music from the past and present. There are hundreds of women's stories from centuries ago and I wanted to share them.

Brazil is a great part of who I am and the artist that I am today.

I really hope we can move faster in fighting inequality in music. I wish we could move faster in fighting inequality in all sectors, but music is my life. I want to invite people to be curious. I want to invite people who listen to the radio to go to concerts, and for them to know that there is a whole world of women in music whose stories have not been properly told. I hope that, with this project, I can inspire.

In my career, I don't feel much inequality because in opera you are hired to sing female and male roles. But that's not a reality for the majority of women in music, as instrumentalists or conductors or directors. I would like to see women receiving equal recognition. More than that, I would like to see no difference. We have to call them *'women composers'* because if you just say *'composer'* people assume it's a man. I would like that to change.

What gives me confidence is being 200 per cent prepared for everything, and remembering that authenticity is the ultimate goal, not perfection.

One of the best pieces of advice that I've been given is, if somebody says something bad about you in a review, remember that's just one person and if somebody says something good, remember that's just one person. There is no finish line when you are an artist; you grow as an artist as you do a person. If you feel in doubt, take a moment to learn, reset and then do what you do with dedication. When you have talent there is this assumption that you never feel insecure, and this is not true. We all have moments of imposter syndrome. What gives me confidence is being 200 per cent prepared for everything, and remembering that authenticity is the ultimate goal, not perfection.

I left Brazil in 2001, when I got a scholarship at the Royal College of Music. I was excited to move to London and develop my repertoire and my career, so it was a moment of great joy. Of course, when I arrived, not everything was easy. It was a culture shock. I was still very Brazilian. When I had my first lessons at the Royal College of Music, I hugged and kissed all my teachers. That was not what they expected! I moved too much; I talked a lot, which was not very good for a classical singer as you should save your voice. I wanted to blend in at the beginning, I wanted to become more English and that was a mistake.

The moment I decided not to blend in was when I really found myself and embraced who I am and where I come from. Brazil is a great part of who I am and the artist that I am today. I was born in a beautiful country. Brazilians are kind and generous people – they fill you with warmth, and that is a crucial part of who I am. When you grow up in Brazil, you see people dealing with adversity on a daily basis, you see people doing that with creativity and a smile on their faces. That is something that stays with you and that I treasure. I know a great part of my resilience, the ability that I have to deal with obstacles when they appear, is down to the fact that I was born in Brazil.

Gabriella's object

I used to play with a toy piano when I was a child. It belonged to my mother and was my first connection with classical music. I used to play it in my bedroom and imagine myself playing concerts all over the world. We couldn't afford a piano, so the toy fed my dreams. The piano is a reminder of the child that I was, and also of my commitment to become somebody who can inspire other young girls who want to do things that might not feel achievable. As an artist, as a woman, there is nothing better than that. One of the best decisions I have made is to use my voice to make a difference when I am off stage. I want to become what that girl on the toy piano needed to help her to fight for her dream.

DR SHINI SOMARA

Dr Shini Somara (born Shini Somarathne) is a mechanical engineer, broadcaster, and author. She has presented *TechKnow* on Al Jazeera America; hosted two educational series of physics and engineering videos on the *Crash Course* YouTube channel; and presented various shows on BBC America, Sky Atlantic, BBC1, BBC2, and PBS. Somara studied Mechanical Engineering at Brunel University before completing an Engineering Doctorate (EngD) in 2003. Her thesis was on Computational Fluid Dynamics, where computer simulations are used to visualise how gases and liquids flow, which helps engineers to design better machines. She hosts a podcast, *Scilence*, and has written a series of STEM books for younger readers, the first in this series is called *An Engineer Like Me*.

My dad is an engineer. He was my inspiration for getting into engineering, always encouraging us to figure out how things work. He's Sri Lankan, my mother is Malaysian, and I have two younger sisters. As the eldest child I always felt I should be flying the flag for engineering.

The perception when I was young was that girls don't do engineering, but I wasn't aware of that. It was only when I got to university that I realised I was in a minority. There were 139 of us in the class and nine of us were girls. Being one of the few women meant I had to try harder. There was more pressure to prove oneself because there was always this assumption that women might struggle. It never really put me off because I am competitive and I worked hard. I wanted to prove that engineering is not a subject purely for men.

My ambition was to take over my dad's company, but careers are like a series of stepping-stones and sometimes it takes courage to go into different things – writing children's books, working in television, starting a podcast. As a teenager I was shy and introverted and some of the things I've done, like being on television, require me to be the opposite. We live in a world where we care very much about everybody else's opinions. I've had to focus on filtering out all those voices that tell you that you can't do something or maybe you shouldn't try.

Engineers are problem solvers. They're always identifying ways they can make our lives better. I'm still an engineer at heart. When you're trying to communicate, there's a problem that needs to be solved. How do we make this content interesting and engaging?

Being a woman as well as a person of colour in a very male-dominated homogenous industry did make me feel uncomfortable, but I was prepared because I'd always felt like that. If you walk with a limp, you get used to walking with a limp. I was limping about, psychologically; I'd learned to live with it. But the times we're living in now mean that I'm able to be easier on myself, to say: *'You have a right to be here.'*

People are starting to embrace difference, to acknowledge that diversity is good for business, as it is for people's wellbeing. There were times that I felt that growing up in a Sri Lankan household was a disadvantage, whereas today I see having a different perspective as an advantage.

Shini's object
These pointe shoes represent a time when I was very disciplined and dedicated to learning something very different to engineering. Classical ballet was physically tough, but also graceful and inspiring. Ballet taught me to carry myself with strength and poise.

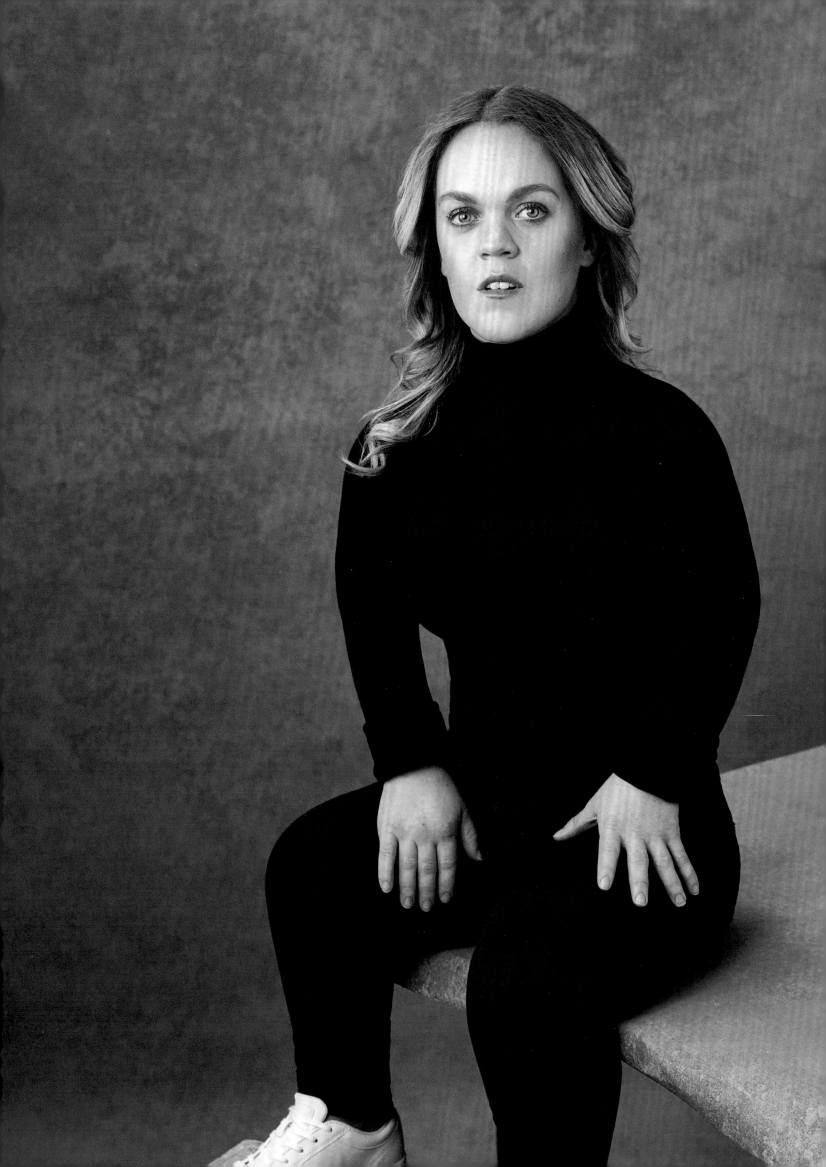

Swimming is my mental freedom.

ELLIE SIMMONDS

Ellie Simmonds, who was born with achondroplasia (dwarfism), was 13 years old when she won two gold medals at the Beijing 2008 Paralympic Games, making her the second youngest British Paralympian to win a medal. She won the BBC's *Young Sports Personality of the Year* award in the same year. In February 2009 she became the youngest person ever to be appointed MBE and later that year won six gold medals and a silver at the IPC Swimming World Championships. At the 2012 Paralympics in London, she not only won two gold, one silver and one bronze medal, but also broke two world records. She was appointed OBE in 2013 for services to Paralympic sport, and won her fifth gold medal at the Rio Paralympics in 2016.

I grew up in Aldridge in Walsall, where my family home is. My family are absolutely amazing. We're very family orientated and we do things together. School was a happy time. I always wanted to be doing lots of things. Even now I get FOMO – fear of missing out!

When I was around eight or nine, I was watching the Athens 2004 Paralympics, and an athlete called Nyree Lewis won the gold medal. That was the turning point. My dream was created: to go to a Paralympics and get a gold medal. Swimming became competitive for me. At 10 I was selected to be part of the British Para-Swimming programme.

When I went to Beijing in 2008, I didn't realise I was a kid. Now I look at 13-year-olds and I think *'Gosh, you guys are young!'* But when I was 13 and going to China for a month to represent Great Britain, I didn't realise how big it actually was. In a sense, that was a great thing, as I didn't feel the pressure; it wasn't that daunting. I was able to just go out there and race: do my thing, swim, and enjoy it. I think that's what helped me get those two gold medals. I remember snippets; being so excited, in awe of everything and how incredible it was. The Olympic village was so big and I was meeting so many people.

Coming back from Beijing was strange. People knew who I was. All I wanted to do was go back to school. I've been really lucky that, throughout my career, my friends and family, everyone around me, has been super-supportive. They keep me grounded. The opportunities that swimming has helped me get – working in the media, meeting lots of amazing people, being on TV – have been absolutely incredible, but I'm also just a normal person going about my business.

I'm proud to say I'm a Paralympian.

As an athlete, you're always looking for the next step. I'm a very driven person. As soon as we touched down from Beijing in 2008, the talk was London 2012. Having a home Paralympics is so special. I knew from my first Games that I wanted to be a better athlete and push myself. I wanted to feel what it was like to be on the podium again and again. It was so exciting to have that build-up to those Games, such a motivation. Yes, you get those days when you can't be bothered. But being an athlete in any sport, it's your life, it's what you dedicate yourself to. Swimming is very time-consuming. We wake up at silly o'clock to train and in the afternoon we go back to the pool. You sometimes want to be that normal person who can lie in a bit longer, and go out. But you have to conquer those days. London 2012 was one of the highlights of my career. That summer got the whole nation together. It was incredible. There are no words to describe it: walking out in front of 17,500 people cheering for you, and coming away with two gold medals, a silver and a bronze, and personal bests – it was a summer of great memories.

London 2012 was a turning point for the Paralympics and the Paralympic movement. Even in the short time I've been around, the Paralympic Games have changed and are moving forwards. The acceptance and awareness are absolutely incredible. I'm proud to say I'm a Paralympian and I tell everyone the Paralympics is a force to be reckoned with. As athletes, we are the same as the Olympians. We train as hard. Every single Paralympic athlete behind that starting block or on the playing field has a story of how they got there. Everyone is individual and they are incredible athletes and human beings. I'm so excited to see where the Paralympics is going to go in the future. London 2012 was also a trigger for awareness of people with disabilities, and their acceptance in society. Changes are happening and things are getting better and better.

After the Rio Paralympics in 2016, I was struggling with a lot of things. At that stage, as a 21-year-old, I wanted to be free. I wanted to figure myself out as a human being and as a woman, and what I wanted to do in life. I decided to take a break and go travelling in 2017. It was one of the best years of my life. I was able to find myself, get confident and be OK on my own. It was also the chance to say yes to things.

Previously in my career, I'd had to say no to things like going to weddings, catching up with friends, and that year I said yes to absolutely everything. Taking a break definitely gave me an insight into what I wanted to do and who I was as an individual.

The best advice I've ever received is to be happy.

I decided to come back to the sport and give it one last shot at Tokyo 2020. As a kid, I always wanted to go to four Games and knew I had one last Games in me. So I thought, *'Come on El! Get in the water, do what you love.'* I realised why I love swimming – it relit the fire in me.

Four months out of the water because of Covid lockdown made me appreciate how much swimming is my mental freedom. It's the sense of being in my own head, of being one with the water, submerged in quietness. Meditation has become a huge thing for me – having that space for your own self and who you are as an individual. The best advice I've ever received is to be happy. My coach always says, *'A happy swimmer is a fast swimmer.'* And finding your happiness can sometimes be quite hard. You've got to discover what makes you happy, but once you do, you can enjoy every single thing.

Ellie's object

My object is my diary. I'm very organised, not just in sport and swimming but also in my personal life. Knowing what I'm going to do each day is something I take comfort in. I take my diary everywhere. It's a comfort blanket for me. My medals are amazing and significant, but, in a sense, now they're just pieces of metal at my parents' house. The whole process around a Paralympics is the memories I hold – the joyful moments, being with people, the photos, and the things that I've achieved.

TWIGGY

Photography by Brian Aris

The photographer said:
'If you do ever decide to be
a model, that would be
a great name.'

TWIGGY

Dame Twiggy Lawson is an actress, singer, designer, and was the world's first supermodel. She began her modelling career at the age of 16, and is a world famous, multi-award winning, fashion icon. She designed her first *Twiggy* collection of clothes in the 1960s and continues to design numerous collections around the world. She won two Golden Globe Awards for her leading role in the film of *The Boy Friend* (1970) and was nominated for a Tony Award for *Best Actress in a Musical* for her Broadway debut in *My One and Only* (1983). Twiggy has recorded numerous best-selling albums. In the mid 2000s she was a judge on *America's Next Top Model*. She was made a Dame of the British Empire in 2019.

It's so funny that I ended up doing what I did because, in our family album, there are photographs of my two elder sisters at tap class and ballet class and at parties. My mum took me to all of those and I wouldn't stay. I'd run out and hold her hand and insist on going home with her. I must have been a pain: all I wanted was to be with my mum. So, it's weird I ended up as a performer.

I had a nice, ordinary, happy, loving family. My dad worked as a master carpenter at film studios, building sets. My mum was a mum. We lived in north-west London and I was spoilt to death because I had two older sisters. I came along seven years after the younger one and 15 years after the older one. I was very, very loved.

Even if you do something and it's not a hundred percent successful, it doesn't matter.

My plan was to go to art college and do fashion and design because I was obsessed with clothes. In those days, you learned to sew: my sisters made their own clothes and so did my mum, partly because it was cheaper – and when I was a teenager, I was a mod, which was a very specific way of dressing.

At weekends I had a Saturday job in a hairdressers where my sister worked. On Sundays my friends would come over and we'd muck about with makeup, and that's

how I started doing the makeup that became synonymous with me. A friend of a friend who worked on a magazine came into the salon and suggested I get some test shots done, and I was sent off to a posh West End hair salon called The House of Leonard.

Leonard wanted to try out his new haircut on me. I was too shy to say no, so I just nodded. And then they sent me off to a photographer, Barry Latigan. At the time I had a boyfriend whose brother had nicknamed me Twiggy because of my legs and my friend said *'Twiggy'* in the studio and the photographer said: *'If you do ever decide to be a model, that would be a great name.'*

He sat me in front of the camera and took what's become an iconic photograph of me in a Fair Isle sweater looking straight to camera. I went back to school with my new haircut and didn't think any more of it. Leonard hung the picture in his salon – and then Deirdre McSharry, a top fashion journalist came in and asked about it, and said she wanted to meet me. Two weeks later I was in the centre of the Daily Express. It was a broadsheet in those days, and it was the whole page, and the headline was: *'Twiggy, the face of 66'* – and that day, my life changed forever.

Within six months I was in Paris doing the collections, and within a year I was in New York with Diana Vreeland, who was the fashion editor of Vogue and the most powerful woman in fashion. She took me under her wing and turned me global. When I first went to America, a documentary was made about my visit which went out on national television. I went to LA and Sonny and Cher threw a party for me on their lawn. It was madness.

My family has always been my safety net because, at home, with them, I'm theirs.

I was very lucky. My dad was down-to-earth, sensible, kind. And he said: *'If you want to do this, you've always got to have somebody with you.'* I was protected. I was close to my parents and I'm close to my sisters and my husband and my children. My family has always been my safety net because, at home, with them, I'm theirs.

It wasn't an ambition to be a model, maybe a distant dream, but in those days working class girls didn't become models. When extraordinary things like that are happening to you, it matters to have your real life. I had my daughter Carly when I was 29 and suddenly you've got this wonderful little child and you're just her mum. She didn't know that I was famous until she was about six or seven. She is still the most important thing in my life along with my husband. I have two grandchildren and all I want is for them to be happy and fulfilled, and the world to be safe for them.

In 1970 Ken Russell cast me as the lead in my first film, *The Boy Friend* (1970). It was an extraordinary experience and changed my career. He was my mentor – and from then on I concentrated on my acting and singing career.

Doing *My One and Only* on Broadway was one of the best professional experiences of my life. I was terrified – but once I overcame the fear, performing in front of a live audience felt like the ultimate high. At the end, the whole audience, 1,500 people, would be up on their feet. Such a huge adrenalin rush, singing and dancing to Gershwin with a 30-piece orchestra. How lucky was I?

My great friend Tommy Tune, who starred with me in *The Boy Friend*, had to work to persuade me to do *My One and Only*. My initial reaction was, *'I can't do that'* – as I was very nervous of appearing live on stage. He said: *'There's no such word as can't.'* And that's been very useful life advice – it's amazing what you can achieve with belief and hard work.

Twiggy's object
My object is a beautiful old silver hand mirror with *'AA'* inscribed on the back. It was given to me on my first night of *My One and Only* on Broadway by Ava Astaire. Her dad was Fred Astaire, who was my idol. I met him in America in the early seventies and through him I met Ava, who lived in London, and we became friends. The mirror had belonged to her aunt, Adele Astaire, who was Fred's first dance partner. I used that mirror every night to put on my makeup for *My One and Only*, and I know it helped my tap dancing: I used to get the Fred and Adele vibes right down to my toes.

TOVA LEIGH

Tova Leigh was born in Israel. She studied law and worked as an employment lawyer for two years before moving to the UK to pursue a career in acting. After getting married and having three children she started her blog, *My Thoughts About Stuff*, sharing her motherhood struggles with other women. The successful blog and vlogs turned her into a social media influencer with over 2 million followers worldwide. Her viral online series *Mom Life Crisis* became a documentary film on Amazon Prime and in 2019 Tova released her first book. Her second book, *You Did WHAT?*, a collection of women's personal stories, was released in 2021.

My ambition as a child was to be a lawyer; I thought that I could do good in the world. But then I became a lawyer and was disillusioned by how little justice there actually was.

I started taking amateur drama classes and I fell in love with acting. At the age of 30 I decided to make a massive change and move to London to pursue acting. Everyone thought I had lost my mind. I was leaving a good career and salary to go and become an actress.

I only ever wanted to stay in the UK for a year to do my masters at drama school. Then I met my now husband, Mike. As clichéd as it sounds, that's why I stayed, and I've been here 16 years.

I had my first daughter when I was 35. For me motherhood didn't come naturally. It's hard to admit that because we are told from an early age that motherhood is our goal. That no matter what else you do, you are going to get to motherhood. That isn't true. Being a mother didn't feel like I thought it would and that was a real shock. I had post-partum depression and only years later did I realise. It's so important to recognise the symptoms.

My twins came less than two years later. Having three children in the space of two years is massive. There aren't words to describe how deeply I felt I was drowning. But there are no people I love more than my daughters; it had nothing to do with them, it was to do with me.

The expectation that the mum drops out of her career to raise the family is a major factor in gender inequality. I automatically stopped work. It was not a conversation we had. Now when I look back, I think *'how did that happen?'*.

One day I snapped and needed to vent. I wrote what ended up being my first blog. Then I started writing on a regular basis and then making vlogs. That's when it kind of exploded.

At first there wasn't a goal in my content, apart from letting mothers, and parents in general, know that they're not alone. I was opening a door for parents to say that they were struggling. I tried to make it funny too and it helped me; it was almost therapeutic. Then my work became more about women. I wanted to break down the boundaries and stereotypes. To say that there's no one way to be a woman or a mother. There is no one way to live your life.

Tova's object

The only object I am genuinely attached to is my phone. It is significant because it's my work, it's my office. But it's a love-hate relationship. On the one hand it has allowed me this amazing opportunity. On the other hand, it represents everything I hate; that constant connection. It is a significant object for good and for bad.

105

ROSEMARY REED

It seems a simple thing, but it's very powerful. If you don't listen, you miss a lot. You can misconstrue what people are saying.

ROSEMARY REED

Rosemary Reed is a producer, director and founder of POW TV (Power of Women TV), a female-led production company. After leaving school without qualifications, she had a varied career before going into talent management and then into production with *Living the Life*, a show on Sky Arts featuring two high-profile figures in conversation. She developed this format for the sports docuseries *Driving Force* and over several series of *Power of Women*, which features two prominent women talking about various topics, from ageism to sustainability, fashion to female empowerment.

I grew up in Covent Garden, where my mum and dad were publicans. I was born in the sixties when Covent Garden was still a fruit and veg market. It was very different from now. My parents were very extrovert, very much part of the community. It was a colourful life.

My parents came over from Ireland in the sixties. My mum has been the biggest influence on my life. She was incredibly hard-working. She had a pub to run, and kids upstairs, and another job cleaning; she left school at the age of 12. But she taught me and my sister never to take no for an answer. She instilled in us the idea that you can have what you want if you believe you can.

I was dyslexic, which I only found out when I was 11. I lost a lot of my childhood because of my insecurities about my dyslexia. I was reserved at school, and I left when I was 15. My ambition was to work with horses – I'd learned to ride in Hyde Park, on Rotten Row, where I used to look after the horses in exchange for a ride. At the age of 15, I went to work in Hertfordshire, training to be a stunt rider, although I was mainly just looking after the horses. But I did work on the *Black Beauty* TV series.

I got pregnant when I was 19. I didn't have any money at all. I could clean, though. My mum was a really good cleaner. I had six cleaning jobs and I saved up to get my first shop in Covent Garden, when the GLC (Greater London Council) was renting shops to local people at low rents to keep communities together.

I hadn't got a clue, but it was great fun, and I sold the business eventually and made a lot of contacts that led on to my next business, which was salons and spas.

The secret of directing is to listen; and the secret of relationships is to listen.

After that I worked at the Hippodrome doing club nights, and that evolved into talent management. I was an agent for five world champion boxers and some incredible actors and singers. Most management agencies now get involved in production as well, and I was very well connected because of running clubs and so on, so I decided to make Living the Life, filming two prominent people talking to each other. I didn't understand directing but then I saw other people doing it and I thought: *'I could do that.'*

In 2009, *Living the Life* was bought by Sky and it was Critic's Choice in a whole series of newspapers – the Times, the Guardian, Observer – and I thought: *'Oh my God, here I am, I can hardly spell; I used to have six cleaning jobs and a baby, and now here I am getting Critic's Choice.'*

There still aren't that many women directing in television. Women aren't usually given the opportunity to be leader of the pack. There is a pack and, if you aren't part of it, you won't get the opportunities. You've got to fight for what you want. I come from quite a hardcore Irish background.

We weren't wallflowers. We knew how to stand up for ourselves.

It's not enough to want success; you must need it.

I've always been very driven. Perhaps it's because I wanted to prove others wrong about my capabilities. I had a Cockney accent and I didn't have the education that I presumed you needed to be successful. But I did grow up in theatreland and I was at home in that world. And I wanted to prove to myself that I could be successful.

The women I've worked with on *Power of Women* and *Driving Force* and my other shows are leaders in their fields. They're all very different but I've noticed a common denominator. They believe in themselves, and that they're going to succeed. It's not enough to want success; you have to need it. Running a business is not a six or seven hours a day commitment. If you're going to see it through, to be proud of what you've done, it has to be 22 hours a day.

A director I worked with who was very highly respected gave me the best advice I've ever received. He said the secret of directing is to listen; and the secret of relationships is to listen. Listening is something I wasn't always very good at before. It seems a simple thing, but it's very powerful. If you don't listen, you miss a lot. You can misconstrue what people are saying.

Of course, I've had plenty of negative comments along the way: *'You're a big mouth. You're a bully. You're this, you're that, you're premenstrual.'* Nothing I couldn't deal with. Frankly, I don't pay attention.

When I made *Driving Force*, I was really shocked by the amount of abuse suffered by female elite athletes and the lack of support they got. And that led to *Power of Women*, which after three seasons I think is really

coming into its own. The stories these women tell speak volumes: Jane Goodall, Baroness Helena Kennedy, Gloria Allred, Twiggy, Mary Quant, Elaine Paige... such a diversity of careers. I forgot I was directing at times because I was just thinking: *'Oh my goodness me, this is amazing! What I'm hearing is amazing!'*

I've got a lot of contacts – a network – and that, I think, is part of my personality, the Irishness in me. I'm quite chatty. I like to hear what people have got to say. I believe it's important to share your contacts. What goes around comes around: if people are decent, they'll come back and support you one day. But it's not only about that. As women we have to help each other. You have to be generous.

Rosemary's object
I have just started a course to become a pastor with Hillsong Church. When I became a born-again Christian, a friend of mine gave me this bible. I keep it by my bed and I read it every day. It represents a new beginning for me. It's a children's bible because my friend knew that, with my dyslexia, reading certain things would confuse me. So the bible has pictures and I love it. I wouldn't swap it for any other kind.

MORAG ROSS

Morag Ross is an award-winning make-up artist who has worked with many film stars including Cate Blanchett, Julie Christie, Bill Murray and Tilda Swinton. At 28 she designed the make-up for her first feature film, Caravaggio, which was released in 1986. Her subsequent work includes the movies *Orlando* (1992), *Sense and Sensibility* (1995), *The Aviator* (2004), *Hugo* (2011), *Carol* (2015), *Cinderella* (2015), *Ocean's Eight* (2018) and the 2020 mini-series *Mrs. America*. She won BAFTAs for her make-up design on *Orlando* and *The Aviator*.

I grew up in Glasgow, Scotland. My father was Scottish and my mother, Indonesian, and I grew up listening to Dutch and Indonesian being spoken in the house, which gave me a love of languages.

When I was at secondary school, I decided that I was going to go to university and study languages. At the very last minute, my art teacher suggested that I apply to art college. So I applied and changed paths, going to Glasgow School of Art.

You will get a lot further in any industry, if you are nice with everyone around you.

I had a great time at art school: punk had just happened and the New Romantics were a huge influence on me and my friends. I got into make-up and did more work on my face than on canvas! At college I specialised in mural design and we were encouraged to have extra-curricular activities. So I volunteered to do art make-up for hairdressing shoots and shows and I loved it.

I did my first film as a make-up designer on Derek Jarman's Caravaggio about the life of the painter. Derek was an amazing filmmaker and painter. That film was beautiful, so it was a great springboard. Derek was a nurturing, generous-minded, gentle person and a great mentor for all who worked for him.

Every job comes with a set of problems to solve, creative issues to be worked out and designed. There are always going to be unknowns and that is a fantastic part of the job, because you learn things along the way.

Jeff Goldblum once said, *'It's nice to be important but it's important to be nice'* and it's true. You will get a lot further in any industry, if you are nice to everyone around you. Being a good make-up artist is a combination of personality and creativity. You have to make somebody feel at ease and confident so that they can inhabit their character and do their work.

I get satisfaction from collaborating with other creative minds towards a great final goal and I love the travel. The hours can be gruelling, so you have to have stamina and commitment, and in film, because there is a lot of money invested, there is pressure to deliver every day.

When you are self-employed it is important to love what you do. If you are going to follow your dream and possibly live in a precarious way, you need a certain amount of passion for it and have support from the people around you.

Morag's object
My mother's Max Factor lipstick from the 1960s in its original gold coloured case is called Firebrand, and it's a beautiful red. I keep the lipstick in my make-up kit as a good luck charm. The pungent waxy smell is evocative – it combines childhood and remembering my mum.

LADY NICOLA MENDELSOHN

*Fear is often the thing
that holds us back. If you
can let go of that, it will
liberate you to do the most
extraordinary things.*

LADY NICOLA MENDELSOHN

Lady Nicola Mendelsohn CBE is Vice President of *Facebook* for Europe, the Middle East and Africa. The Daily Telegraph named her *'Most Powerful Woman in the Tech Industry'*. Before Facebook she worked for 20 years in advertising and in 2011 became the first female president of the Institute of Practitioners in Advertising. In 2016 Mendelsohn was diagnosed with follicular lymphoma. She founded the Follicular Lymphoma Foundation in 2019, with the sole purpose of finding a cure for this incurable blood cancer.

I grew up in Manchester surrounded by family. I've got two younger brothers and it was a busy and happy household and I have a lot of fond memories of playing with friends from our neighbourhood after school in the street. Entrepreneurialism was a theme in my life from an early age – my grandma ran a haberdashery business and my mum still runs a catering firm.

At university I studied English and drama. Theatre is one of my passions and I thought seriously about becoming an actor, but ultimately I decided to go into advertising. It wasn't a career I'd heard a lot about growing up. But luckily, I had a friend who had gone into the industry who inspired me to pursue it. At the end of university, I applied for a graduate trainee scheme at the agency Bartle, Bogle & Hegarty (BBH) in London – and was accepted.

Since the pandemic there's been a seismic shift in the way that people think about working practises. There's absolutely no reason why you shouldn't be able to work flexibly and remotely.

It was an incredibly exciting time to be in advertising. BBH had just come out with their groundbreaking Levi's *'Launderette'* ad, and the founders of the firm were trailblazers in the industry. John Bartle took me under his wing and gave me opportunities for leadership early on. He is a true ally and I'll always be grateful to him.

I spent 20 years in advertising, and I learned so much during that time: what a great campaign looks like, how to be there for your clients, how to build the perfect pitch. The thing I love most about advertising is that there is so much innovation. It brings together the best of business and the best of creativity. It was a career that took me all over the world, and I absolutely loved it.

In 2013, Facebook approached me for the role of Vice President for Europe, the Middle East and Africa. I saw it as a fantastic opportunity to represent an incredibly diverse region, stretching from South Africa all the way to Scandinavia. I've been at Facebook for eight years now, and no two days are the same. I regularly meet with businesses both big and small who use our platforms and with Facebook community leaders and creators. Before the pandemic you would find me on a plane travelling all over the world, but now all of this is virtual – I've even hosted my first client event in virtual reality!

The world of work has changed so much since I started in my career. Back then, it was unusual for a woman to return to the ad industry after having one child – and I had four! For 16 years, I made this work by working a four-day week. My bosses at BBH and Grey gave me this flexibility, and it allowed me to continue advancing my career. Today, we're seeing a seismic shift in the way that people think about work. I think that's healthy, and a good thing. There's absolutely no reason why you shouldn't be able to work flexibly and remotely.

There's a very clear issue in the tech industry that we don't have enough women, and it's an issue that all of us need to do something about. There's an onus on all of us to encourage young girls to think about taking STEM subjects. I'm really pleased that at Facebook, we're moving upwards in terms of women in senior leadership positions and women in engineering. But we still have a lot of work to do. It's absolutely fundamental that we have diversity across all parts of the company. It's the right thing to do, and it makes business sense. Companies that are more diverse are more successful.

The woman that most inspires me is Sheryl Sandberg – I'm lucky to have her as a colleague and as a friend. Sheryl cares deeply about helping women to thrive in the workplace. She's not somebody that pulls the ladder up behind her. She throws ladders down because she wants more and more women to succeed.

There are many moments that I've been incredibly proud of in my life. From a work perspective, it was an unbelievable privilege to open the first Facebook office on the African continent. I'll also never forget the day I went with my family to Buckingham Palace to receive a CBE from Her Majesty the Queen! It was one of the most extraordinary days. But when I think back on my life, the thing I'm absolutely most proud of is my family. Even saying the word family makes me smile.

In 2016, I was diagnosed with an incurable blood cancer - follicular lymphoma. At the time of diagnosis, I was feeling totally well, running a busy career and family. So the diagnosis was a complete shock. The weekend I heard was the worst of my life. I hit rock bottom. But after that, I decided that I wouldn't let the cancer control my life.

Follicular lymphoma isn't a well-known cancer – I'd never heard of it before my diagnosis. Treatments for it haven't advanced much for

decades. That's why I created the Follicular Lymphoma Foundation in November 2019 (theflf.org). Its sole purpose is to find a cure for the hundreds of thousands of people that are living with this cancer around the world.

If I were to give advice to my younger self, I'd say – do the things you think you can't do! Take yourself out of your comfort zone. Those are the moments where you learn the most, and feel a real sense of achievement. I would also tell my younger self that when you're in a meeting, you are valuable, your voice matters, and therefore you should trust your instincts and speak up more. Fear is often the thing that holds us back. If you can let go of that, it will liberate you to do the most extraordinary things.

Nicola's object

My significant object is my pair of Shabbat candles. The candles were given to me by my grandmother and one day I will give them to my daughter. I light them every Friday night on the eve of the Jewish Sabbath. It's a moment of reflection where I can embrace my religion and bring God into my life. It's a moment where I take prayer. It's a silent meditation and it connects me to the many thousands of years of Judaism, which is such a fundamental part of my life.

RACHEL SINGER

Rachel Singer is a tailor who specialises in women's bespoke tailoring. After studying Graphic Design she went on to study bespoke tailoring at The Savile Row Academy and was then taken on as a coat maker at Maurice Sedwell on Savile Row. Her role expanded to include pattern cutting, fitting and training others in bespoke tailoring. She studied and experimented with women's bespoke tailoring in her own time. In 2019, she won *The Golden Shears Tailoring Competition* with her womenswear entry. She has since set up her own bespoke tailoring business, making her one of the few female tailors in a field where women are significantly under-represented.

I grew up in south-west London. I have an interesting family because even though neither of my parents work in the clothing industry, all of the women on my mum's side are fantastic seamstresses and on my dad's side they had a haberdashery and my grandfather had a shoe making company.

When I was seven, my mum was pregnant with my little sister and I remember she started knitting her cardigans. She took an ordinary ball of string and transformed it into this extraordinary garment. I thought it was magic. I started with making clothes for my sister's Barbie dolls and then I moved onto making outfits for myself, quite bonkers outfits. I loved playing around with how I looked.

I was convinced I was going to do a fashion degree and go onto be a fashion designer. I didn't know what a job in sewing looked like, and as far as I could tell a fashion degree didn't lead directly to making clothes. I knew I wanted to have a career where I was making something with my hands. I decided to do a graphic design degree, which enabled me to work with people, in a way that didn't seem to be possible in fashion.

Out of university, I was thinking about what I wanted to do, how I wanted to work and then it just occurred to me – why am I not sewing? Why am I not finding a way for sewing to be part of my daily life? It was after I graduated that I decided to specialise in tailoring and started my training on Savile Row. It really was a penny drop moment.

I love my job and I love what I do. My job doesn't involve sitting at a desk in front of a computer all day. I stand at my work bench with an iron in one hand, a thimble on the other and I make clothes all day. When I'm not tailoring, I knit, I do woodwork or build brick walls. I always feel my best when I'm making something.

If I could speak to my younger self I would say stop wasting time hating your body so much. I spent years not liking how I looked. When I was younger, everyone in fashion magazines were desperately thin with blonde hair. I knew I wasn't that. Today I think it's very different, brilliantly so. There is much more diverse representation of beauty these days, but there is still a really long way to go.

Studying tailoring was almost a therapy for understanding my own body. When we buy clothes, it's about our body fitting into those clothes, whereas with tailoring it's about those clothes fitting your body, no matter what shape or size. For me, being able to make my own clothes that fit me, that are comfortable, has made me learn to love my body. And now I want to help other women love their bodies too.

Rachel's object

My thimble is only very small but it plays a really essential role. It enables me to work with my hands all day. It symbolises me making a commitment to be a tailor. It's like a doctor wearing a stethoscope. It symbolises everything I have achieved.

SUE HANNAM

Sue Hannam is the first female head teacher of Lichfield Cathedral School – an independent day school in Staffordshire established in 1942 but with a lineage that traces back to the 14th century. She completed a degree in English Language and Literature, studied in part at the University of Innsbruck, Austria; an MA in the Political Economy of the Media Industry, and a Postgraduate Certificate in Education (PGCE) from Birmingham University. She went on to qualify as a solicitor, then returned to teaching. In 2009, she was recruited to establish a new sixth form at Lichfield Cathedral School where she was made head in 2015. In 2019 she *'travelled through time'* as the Head Teacher in the BBC History Series *'Back in Time For School'* and can often be seen as an education commentator on television news channels.

When I was at school, I had a conversation with my mum about being a medical or legal secretary because that seemed to be what you did when you were a young girl in north Birmingham. The deputy head, who was a feisty, fabulous woman, called my parents in and said, *'Why do you want Sue to be the spanner if she can be the mechanic?'* That analogy fundamentally changed the route of my life.

I was the first person in my family to go to university. I got an English degree and wanted to be a lawyer. The plan was that I would teach for one year and then do the law conversion. What happened was, I taught for a year and I really rather liked it. I taught for another year and then another and thought, *'If I don't leave now, I never will.'* I did the law conversion and then spent two years doing a training contract with a firm of solicitors and qualifying. I learned all sorts of utterly invaluable things and one of the biggest lessons was that my heart lay in the education of children.

Just because you set off on one track, it doesn't mean you are a single-track pony. If you are too blinkered, it's easy to lose sight of the opportunities that are coming, perhaps from left field, and that can be where the real treasures lie.

I began teaching in 1995 and, when I reflect on the first few years of my career, I think young people have always had a sense of altruism and a social conscience and there was always a sense of them wanting to do good. Young people are often undervalued in our society. People talk about youths in a disparaging way. Well, you know what? Youth is hope and our future. Every single day, I see good deeds, phenomenal ideas, true humanity, real compassion, and a total lack of bigotry and prejudice from young people. If you get a group with a heartfelt sense of direction, they can move mountains. Working with young people is a job that gives you hope, because they are phenomenal.

Sue's object
I recently found a strip of photographs of my grandmother as a young woman. She was born in 1904, she was not always in good health, not blessed with lots of money and she had to work really hard, but she was the most joyful person. She is captured in a moment, the embodiment of fun, irrespective of everything that would have been going on: the two world wars that she lived through, working in service as a cook, not having an easy life. She was so influential to me and she was a bibliophile – she read and read. She is why I ended up with an English degree and I thank her very much. When I found these photos, I realised in how many ways I am her and she is me, and that is really special.

DR JESS WADE

Jess Wade is a physicist who studies new materials at Imperial College London, where she earned both her MSc and PhD, having previously studied art at Chelsea College of Art. Outside of the lab, Jess is involved with several initiatives focused on improving diversity in science. She spends her evenings researching and writing the Wikipedia biographies of scientists and engineers from historically marginalised groups, and has written one every single day since the beginning of 2018. Jess has received several awards for contributions to communication, diversity and inclusion, and in the 2019 *Queen's Birthday Honours* she received a BEM.

Both my parents and brother are medical doctors and we spoke about science all the time. Throughout my childhood, science, discovery and curiosity were all seen as cool things to be interested in.

I was a bit of a nerd at school. I studied maths, further maths, chemistry, physics and art. My teachers really brought sciences and arts together and emphasised how important creativity was in the sciences, and how scientific thinking was also in the arts. It really shaped the scientist I became.

Science has this image problem where it's not attracting or inspiring enough young people to study it. We need to make science a career and speciality where women and people of colour and the LGBQT+ scientists feel as valued as their white male counterparts. Science is massively missing out from having such a homogeneous group of people doing it.

Angela Saini's book *Inferior* is probably the most powerful book I've ever read. It looks at how biased people and biased scientists have impacted the way that women have progressed and become leaders in all different kinds of disciplines. I read the book in 2017, and it completely transformed my activism and the way I think about inequality. It made me much more vocal about what we needed to do to support women and other minorities in Science. I suddenly realised I can do this: I can change it and I can make sure other people read this too.

I got a lot louder in all of my activism. I learnt that we need to get better at documenting the stories of women making incredible discoveries and standing up to the oppressive regimes in society. For the last three years I have been writing the Wikipedia biographies of women and people of colour working in STEM, to make sure these stories are documented. The reality is that 80-90 percent of the editors are men, and 83 per cent of the biographies are about men. It is such an important platform for education and documenting our history that it is crucial it is impartial and unbiased.

Women's work needs to be valued and recognised. I don't think women or men need to change, but the metrics by which we evaluate people and promote them are really skewed in men's favour and we should re-think that whole process.

Jess's object
In 2018 I set up a crowdfunding page to get a copy of *Inferior* into every high school in the UK. Within 12 days we had raised enough money to get it into every high school library. I love the idea that for years to come, these books will be sitting in school libraries waiting for that little girl or boy to discover, read and learn why we need to keep up this fight for equality.

I THINK
REAL CHANGE
HAPPENS WHEN WE
WORK AS A COLLECTIVE
AND WITH
REGARD TO
GENDER EQUALITY,
NO ONE IS
EQUAL
UNTIL WE'RE ALL EQUAL.

ELIZABETH NYAMAYARO

SOCIETY

Challenging limiting stereotypes, bias and systems. Championing diversity and representation.

Gender inequality has real consequences for society as a whole and for every individual. Violence against women, objectification and discrimination are a danger to women's lives, and to their mental and physical health. Across the world the day-to-day, subtle forms of sexism can negatively impact a woman's sense of well-being and success. This bias is even more oppressive when we consider intersectionality in the forms of race, disability, sexual orientation and religion.

Many of the women interviewed in this book have become passionate activists fighting to make the necessary changes to achieve equity and reduce the mental and physical burden on all oppressed groups. They see the interplay between women's place in the world and so many of the problems that we face globally – climate change, poverty, racial and social inequality.

These heroic women know that inequality not only affects the lives of individuals, but also stunts economic growth and hinders development. Women not only bear the brunt of poverty, but their empowerment is also central for its elimination. And they know that we must work together, and do our own part, to ensure a brighter future for all.

Do not wait for someone else to come and speak for you. It's you who can change the world.
MALALA YOUSAFZAI

GINA MARTIN

What I find satisfying about activism is being part of something that's much bigger than myself.

GINA MARTIN

Gina Martin is a British political activist and author. She is known for her campaign to make upskirting illegal in England and Wales, which led to the 2019 Voyeurism (Offences) Act. She went on to publish a book, *Be The Change: A Toolkit for the Activist in You*. In 2019, she was included in the BBC's *100 Women* and Time Magazine's *100 Next* lists; and named *Equality Champion of the Year* at the Stylist *Remarkable Women Awards* and *Disruptor/Changemaker of the Year* at the Cosmopolitan Magazine *Influencer Awards*. In 2020, she rejected an OBE, citing concerns about the '*violence and oppression*' of the British Empire.

My family are all Liverpudlian. They are funny, silly and don't take themselves seriously. My dad is a session drummer; my mum an interior designer. We travelled for my dad's job and my parents were more open-minded than some in the small rural town in Cheshire where I grew up. They taught me to be a good person and to use my voice.

I was bullied quite badly in school and didn't have a lot of friends. I would hear, *'Gina's very annoying, Gina's very loud, Gina's a bit weird.'* Those things that were annoying when I was younger are good for what I do now. Being loud and proud and using my voice makes me a good campaigner. I am able to get people to care about something because I don't hold back and censor myself. I think that courage comes from the way I was raised: there was nothing we couldn't talk about, it didn't matter if it was good, bad or uncomfortable.

I didn't have big ambitions at school; I was happy plodding along. I wasn't good at science or maths, but I was creative and loved art and to write. When I was a teenager, I wanted to be an art director. I used to watch adverts, which I saw as short films, and thought I could do better.

By 2017, I was a copywriter working in advertising in London. I went to a family festival called British Summer Time in Hyde Park with my sister. We were standing in the crowd in the middle of the day, waiting for a band to come on stage, and a group of guys were hitting on us. After about 45 minutes,

one of them made a loud, crude joke about me and, a couple of minutes later, he stuck his phone between my legs and took photos up my skirt. I didn't see him do it, but I heard him laughing and, when I looked round, a group of guys I didn't know were looking at photos of my crotch on WhatsApp.

I'd had a gin – maybe two – and I thought, *'No! Not this again.'* I hadn't been upskirted before but there had been loads of moments when I had been made to feel out of control of my own body, or disempowered by someone else's comments and made to feel small or scared or sexualised. So I grabbed the phone and held it up and he and I got into a bit of a fight – well, I slapped him and cried. My sister helped me to get away and I ran through the crowd with his phone. He chased me but I got to security, gave them the phone and they called the police. The police came and said, *'It's not a nice photo but it's not a graphic image, so we can't do much.'*

Everyone thinks it's a prank and, actually, it's not a joke, it's a sexual offence.

I could have prosecuted, but it would have been incredibly difficult because upskirting didn't exist in law as an offence. I decided to take it as far as I could in law. It was about kicking up a fuss. This stuff is happening all the time and it's so normalised. Everyone thinks it's a prank and, actually, it's not a joke, it's a sexual offence. I couldn't exist in a public place without being sexualised and punished by a guy who was trying to hit on me. He was upset that I'd said no, so he upskirted me.

He was upset that I'd said no, so he upskirted me.

For the campaign, I applied all the principles of advertising. I continued to work full time – I would get up at 5am to work on the campaign. I started with a social media post on Facebook to identify the group of guys. It went viral and I got a lot of abuse, including horrible messages from men saying they wanted to rape me. I was sure that I was going to be kidnapped or hurt. We dehumanise such people and call them trolls, but they serve you coffee, work in your office and are the fathers of girls. I would look at their profiles and there would be a 35-year-old dad holding his daughter at a birthday party with his wife and friends.

During the campaign, I cried all the time – my brain couldn't deal with thousands of people shouting at me through my phone; I was having anxiety attacks and I went into therapy. I also kept expecting the photos of my crotch to be released. To this day, those guys could still have the photos on their phone, which is humiliating, terrifying and repetitively traumatic. I got up every day and did the work but struggled in private. I couldn't stop: the fact that people thought that it was okay to send abusive messages, was the very reason that I had to continue.

For two years, I worked with a lawyer called Ryan Whelan and, in April 2019, we changed the Sexual Offences Act of 2003 to include upskirting, and introduced the Voyeurism Act.

What I find satisfying about activism is being part of something that's much bigger than myself. The purpose is like nothing I've ever felt before, but the struggle is like nothing I've ever felt before. But I can't do anything else. I can't go back to advertising and sell whisky: I just don't care, it's not important to me.

Everybody who does this work is putting themselves on the line, but some are risking far more than me: in many countries, you can't call yourself an activist because you'll get killed.

Now I am really focusing on learning about and discussing the deconstruction of white supremacy, which, with capitalism, is the basis for all the problems we have in society. If we fight the systems that divide us and build coalitions with black and brown communities with compassion and understanding, and give up space for each other, we'll start getting somewhere.

Gina's object

From 2015 I lived in Greece for a year. At the time, my partner was a marine engineer and we lived on a tiny wooden boat. People would come on holiday and we'd look after them at sea – 30 people in 14 boats. Trying to keep people alive at sea is stressful and I painted whenever I had a few hours off. In the end, I started painting the boat and I painted this massive fish on one of the doors. My friend Patrick – the platonic love of my life – still works in Greece and, years later, he got this door, put it in his suitcase, flew back to England and gave it to me for my birthday. The door represents a time in my life when I didn't really own anything or have contact with the internet, and I was with the two men that I love more than anything. It's like before times, and it makes me feel calm whenever I look at it.

NADIA MURAD
Photography by Judith Litvine

*I still believe a better
world is possible — that
women can be respected,
protected, and empowered.*

NADIA MURAD

Nadia Murad, *Nobel Peace Prize Laureate* and UNODC Goodwill Ambassador, is a leading advocate for survivors of genocide and sexual violence. Nadia's peaceful life was brutally disrupted in 2014 when ISIS attacked her homeland in Sinjar to ethnically cleanse Iraq of all Yazidis. Since Nadia's escape from ISIS captivity, she has shared her story to raise awareness of ISIS and its genocidal campaign against the Yazidi people and the widespread use of sexual violence in war. Nadia is the President and Chairwoman of Nadia's Initiative, which actively works to persuade governments and international organisations to support the sustainable re-development of the Yazidi homeland. In 2017, Nadia released her memoir, *The Last Girl: My Story of Captivity and My Fight Against the Islamic State*.

I grew up in a small village called Kocho in the Sinjar region of Northern Iraq. Kocho was a shepherd and farming village where Yazidi families have lived for generations. As is common in my community, my family was very large. I had eight brothers, two sisters, half-siblings, sisters-in-law, aunts, uncles and cousins. We lived a modest life. Our livelihoods were dependent on our farmlands, so everyone helped my mother with farming duties.

Speaking out was about necessity, not strength.

Growing up, my mother was my world. She taught me to be strong and speak my mind. She was smart, caring, and never stopped working to build a better life for our family. My mother made me who I am today. She taught me about resilience, independence, and courage. I miss her every day.

School was where I first encountered the realities of what it meant to be a marginalised community. Saddam Hussein formed public education in Iraq for the sake of shaping one national Arab identity. This meant that the school system was designed to erase our Yazidi identity. The curriculum was taught in Arabic, even though most Yazidis grew up speaking Kurmanji, a Kurdish dialect. History was always my favourite subject, but our history books never mentioned the existence of Yazidis. Instead, they narrated a violent account of the Iraqi struggle for independence and the legacy of religious wars.

Despite this, I never took school for granted. Education was a luxury that was not easily afforded by families who needed their children to help put food on the table. As the youngest, I was the only one of my siblings who was able to attend school. Everyone else had to work on our farm in order to make ends meet. My family was unable to send me to secondary school until one was built in our village, because it was too expensive to send me to the nearest school. Still, I was dedicated to learning. I felt empowered in school and hoped that my generation might one day be able to teach our own history.

On 3 August 2014, ISIS attacked the Yazidis in Sinjar. They killed the men and took the women and girls. I survived horrific events at the hands of ISIS before I escaped. Watching the suffering of my community for seven years has been painful. Hundreds of thousands of Yazidis are still displaced, thousands of women and children are still held captive by ISIS, and our existence continues to be threatened by the region's instability.

I started Nadia's Initiative in 2018 because I wanted to create sustainable solutions for my community's recovery. I advocated for years for global leaders to come to our aid, but I could not wait any longer. Most of the Yazidi community are displaced in camps only a few hours away from their homes. They are unable to return because Sinjar's basic infrastructure – clean water, electricity, roads, schools, houses, farms and hospitals – was destroyed. For many, moving forward will only be possible in their homeland. I want to help create opportunities for displaced Yazidis to safely return home to Sinjar.

For me, speaking out was about necessity, not strength. I believed that stories of the Yazidi experience would have the power to move people to action. The title of my book is *The Last Girl*, because I'd hoped to be the last girl in the world who had to experience rape and genocide. Unfortunately, it did not end with me. Women and girls around the world continue to be targets of ethnic cleansing and sexual violence. But I still believe a better world is possible; that women can be respected, protected and empowered.

My advocacy work is never about prizes or recognition. It has always been about my community's need for justice and support. Initially, I did not want to accept the Nobel Prize because I did not think it would help Yazidis return home or hold ISIS accountable. I worried the world would think the Yazidi struggle was over because I had been awarded this prize. In the end, I accepted it because I hoped the Nobel would help provide a larger platform for raising awareness and resources to help our cause. It helped me to launch Nadia's Initiative and many impactful projects on the ground in Sinjar.

I want people to understand that no one wants to become a refugee. It is incredibly difficult to leave everything you know behind, cross a border, and learn to live in a new place. It is also often the only option for people whose homes have become unlivable due to persecution, poverty, natural disasters and violence. We want to return to our homeland and our communities. We know that foreign countries are not eager to take in more refugees. That is why the sustainable solution

to preserving my community and culture is to invest in local governance, security, and basic services, so Yazidis can live in safety and dignity.

I want to see my community heal. It requires justice, reparations, security, democratic governance, and investment in Sinjar. Perpetrators must be held accountable in courts of law for genocide and sexual violence. Survivors should be compensated for what they lost and empowered to build a brighter future. All of these steps take political will, which is why my advocacy work and the work of other survivors is so critical to ensuring the international community will not forget the plight of the Yazidis.

My significant object is a dress for a friend's wedding in Kocho. This dress represents many things to me. It reminds me of a time long ago, before the violence of genocide swept through my community. In Kocho, my cousin was planning to get married. There was some fabric at home, and I worked with my nieces to make a dress for me to wear at the wedding. But the wedding never happened. ISIS came and destroyed my home and my community. They took my mother and brothers from me. I felt nothing but sadness and despair for a long time.

DEBORAH FRANCES-WHITE

The next stage for feminism is that we put our humanity first and our identity second.

DEBORAH FRANCES-WHITE

Deborah Frances-White is a stand-up comedian, podcaster, screenwriter and activist. In 2015 she started a podcast called *The Guilty Feminist* which went on to win Gold at the British Podcast Awards in 2020. Her book *The Guilty Feminist: From Our Noble Goals to our Worst Hypocrisies* became a Sunday Times bestseller. She has written a film called *Say My Name*; and her live shows – *Cult Following* and *Half a Can of Worms* – were turned into a BBC Radio 4 comedy series for which she won a Writers Guild Award. Deborah is an Ambassador for Amnesty International and Choose Love.

I am from a beach town in Australia. I read a lot and wanted to be a writer. I also wanted to be an actress; I went to after-school drama club and loved performing. I never imagined getting married and having children, but I always imagined going to university.

When I left school I couldn't go to university for religious reasons. Instead I went to live in London – it was where all the stories in my favourite books were set. I loved the bustle of the city and the opportunity to see theatre, ballet and music. When I heard that some other young women had moved to London and had a spare bed in a bedsit, I jumped on a plane.

Once I had drifted away from my religion I applied to Oxford University on a whim. I was doing comedy improvisation and somebody said, *'Oxford would love you.'* I was older than a regular student and had skills: I spoke conversational Japanese; I had learned sign language and worked as an interpreter.

At Oxford, people who had been in school uniform the year before would say things like, *'I think I will direct an opera at the Oxford Playhouse.'* I thought, *'How do you have that confidence?'* Tutorials were in an ancient tower with a spiral staircase. At the top would be the tutor: you had to read your essay out, then he would play devil's advocate and test your mettle. At one point, my tutor was grilling me and I came back with an answer. He said, *'That's a good point, why wasn't that in your essay?'* And I said, *'None of the critics had said it so I wasn't sure it was right.'* My tutor said,

'You are an Oxford scholar, your opinion is as important as any in the world.'

The people in this country who seem entitled have had resources; entitlement is the residue of privilege.

I realised that's why the other students had such confidence, that's why they thought they could direct an opera at 19. If you are told from the age of eight that your opinion is as important as anyone's in the world and, what's more, you're told that in an ancient building that has beautiful architecture and you have your feet up on the desk, it's difficult to be intimidated. The people in this country who seem entitled have had resources; entitlement is the residue of privilege.

Every couple of years, there's a study which says that when a role is advertised, men assess to see if they have around 50 percent of the skills and think, *'I'll go for that. I can learn the other 50 percent on the job.'* Women assess that they need 100 percent of the skills. The same conclusion is always drawn: women should be more confident; women should be like men. I think that men could stop going up for roles for which they are not qualified. Don't go for a job if you can't do it, like President of the United States of America for example. If we see a trend that men are more confident to express opinions, talk over people, volunteer for things that they don't have much experience in, I suggest that they pull back a bit, as we push forward a bit.

In 2015, I noticed that the conversations that I was having with my friends were changing. They were shifting from our careers and triumphs in bed to the state of the nation for women. There was this new wave of feminism and I wanted to be part of it, but I wasn't sure I was good enough.

Feminists in the public eye seemed so strident, so sure of everything. Bridget Christie would do funny, angry rants in her comedy shows, and was successful. She said, *'Deborah, you will never be successful until you say the things you don't dare, that's when you find your audience.'* What I wanted to say was, *'I am a feminist but, I went on a women's rights march, popped into a department store to use the loo, got distracted trying out face cream and, by the time I came out, the march was gone.'* Was I going to find my audience saying that or would I just get kicked out of the feminist club?

I had nothing to lose so I started *The Guilty Feminist* podcast with Sofie Hagen, a comedian from Denmark. We thought that 100 regular listeners would be great. Five years later, we've had 85 million downloads because an awful lot of people feel, *'I am a feminist, but I am not sure that I am doing it right and I want to get better.'*

There was this new wave of feminism and I wanted to be part of it.

My mission when I started was to wallow in my own oppression; what I have learned, more than anything, is about my own privilege. The podcast is an activist space now. At the beginning we were talking about shoes and the way that women are pushed into heels and how that made us feel. We'd talk about advertising and how we felt about our bodies. Now we are much more likely to have a refugee on talking about their experience, and then we'll figure out a campaign to help.

The next stage for feminism is that we put our humanity first and our identity second. When we start to see refugees – male, female, non-binary – as humans first and being a refugee as something that has happened to them, that's when we will address the crisis. We will see it as a human crisis not a crisis of displacement.

Deborah's object
I have a necklace with charms and the one I treasure is the coin that was damaged by the suffragettes as a protest. On the front of the coin, they put *'VOTES FOR WOMEN'* and on the back *'WSPU'*, which stands for *Women's Social and Political Union*. Sometimes the suffragettes blew stuff up, chained themselves to railings or went on hunger strike but there were smaller protests, like damaging – and therefore devaluing – money, that were called *'outrages'*. A real-life suffragette dug those words into the coin because she imagined a better future for me, where I could vote and laws were made for women. I wear this coin as a reminder to be outrageous and to push back, and that people come before profit.

JOYCE BANDA

Photography by the office of the Former President of Malawi

I became aware that girls can fail to continue education through no fault of their own, and it can affect the rest of their lives.

JOYCE BANDA

Joyce Banda was the President of Malawi from 7 April 2012 to 31 May 2014. The founder of the People's Party, created in 2011, she previously served as Malawi's Minister of Foreign Affairs, and was Vice President from May 2009 until she took over as President, following the death of the previous incumbent. A long-time educator and women's rights activist, her initial ministerial roles included responsibility for gender issues, child welfare and community services; she worked to enact domestic violence and child abuse legislation.

When my father started work in the Malawi police force, which was about 15km away from my village, he insisted: *'I want to take my child to town, because I want to send her to school.'* My family argued and argued, and in the end my father won. They agreed that every weekend I would go back to the village so that my grandmother could bring me up and teach me all about being a village woman and a housewife. Every Friday, as I got down from the bus, my best friend from the village, Chrissie, would be waiting for me by the roadside. We'd have fun walking back into the village: she would tell me what had happened during the week while I was away and I would tell her what had happened in town.

Chrissie went to the village school; I went to the urban school. Chrissie was brighter than me – Chrissie was in first position in every class. We were both selected for the best girls' secondary schools in Malawi. I went to *Providence* Secondary School, she went to St Mary's, in different districts. When I came back for the next holiday, Chrissie was not by the roadside, waiting for me. Chrissie's family had failed to raise the $6 that Chrissie required to go back to school. And so, aged 14, I became aware that girls can fail to continue education through no fault of their own, and it can affect the rest of their lives. Thirty-nine million girls in Africa are not in school. And as if that's not enough, since Covid-19, nine million more girls have dropped out.

I had one brother and four sisters. We grew up in a household where my father gave us equal opportunities. He made sure he interacted with us. I was fortunate to grow up in that household. In most African traditions, girls don't talk with their fathers. The father sits behind the house with the other men, and your brother sits there with them. The only radio in the village is with them. On the other side of the house, you are with your mother, and her sisters.

Women make the best leaders because they face challenges, they take risks, and they're fearless, they're sincere and they're compassionate.

I was married at age 21. By age 26, I had three children. I was in an abusive marriage for 10 years. I realised that if I wanted a better life for my three children I needed to make a move. At the time, there was so much pressure to remain married, but I moved out, and went and studied again. I realised that the economic empowerment of women is key. When you are economically empowered, you can provide better nutrition, health and education for your children. By 1985, not only had I married again, but I had grown my business to a level where I was able to make a contribution to the household. When you make a financial contribution, you gain respect.

In 1990, now that I was – by Malawi standards – a rich woman, I looked at all those who were not as fortunate as myself, and I decided to start an organisation called the National

138

Association of Business Women. By 1997, that organisation was the largest rural network for women in Malawi and 50,000 women had been empowered. I received the *Africa Prize for Leadership for the Sustainable End of Hunger*: and I looked at what I could do with the $50,000 that I received as the award money.

I decided my contribution would be to send as many girls as possible to school. I had promised myself this when I was 14 and Chrissie didn't go to school. So I started the Joyce Banda Foundation. The first day, there were only three girls, and now, the Joyce Banda Foundation has sent 6,500 girls to school, and 1,500 to university.

I didn't plan to end up in politics. I believe that leadership is a love affair. You must fall in love with the people and the people must fall in love with you. I fell in love with the rural people and the underprivileged people of this country at a very young age. There's a lot of power in the people there, and, when they love you, they stand for you through thick and thin.

Those of us who are my age must reach out and help the younger ones.

Those of us who are my age must reach out and help the younger ones. We have had so many challenges in our lives; we must provide support to the younger ones so that they don't go the hard way, like we did. If you listen to Julia Gillard, the misogyny in Australia is very similar to the misogyny in Africa. Our challenges have been the same. I always say to African women that they must not get discouraged, because in the whole world women are facing the same challenges. What we need to do it stand up and say, *'Somebody has to do it.'* We cannot chicken out, we cannot say we will not do it and leave our brothers to proceed. I have always said the reason why Africa has done so well in getting women

into positions of leadership, of presidency, is because we have agreed that we will participate in leadership, but we will do it our way: our understanding of feminism must be African. Your understanding of feminism is your own, and we must respect one another.

My task now is to encourage all African women who make it to support younger girls. Women make the best leaders because they face challenges, they take risks, and they're fearless, they're sincere and they're compassionate.

Joyce's object

My significant object is the Malawi flag – my flag. Before I became President, the previous president changed it, and there was an outcry, because, if you look at it, it's the sun, and it's rising – so the feeling we get as Malawians is that we keep rising. The other president took off the rising sun and put a complete sun to say: *'We have developed, we have arrived.'* For me, the flag with the rising sun [which she reinstated] gives me hope and is very significant in my life. It sits on my desk to make me look forward every day and hope for a good future.

MIKA SIMMONS

Mika Simmons is an actress, film-maker and host of her podcast, *The Happy Vagina*, which empowers women to talk about their health and bodies. Mika also started the Lady Garden Foundation, a charity raising awareness of gynaecological cancers. In 2021 she co-founded the Ginsburg Women's Health Board who campaign to close the gender health gap.

I was born in London. My mother was from a very large Irish family and was raised Catholic, but she rebelled against it. My parents were quite political and my mother was a feminist.

After university I had a burning desire to train as an actor, so I headed off to London to do a year at drama school. Just as I was finishing drama school, I went home to see my mother and she told me that she had been diagnosed with ovarian cancer. I didn't know the severity of ovarian cancer – I don't think I'd ever even heard of it. Back then cancer was a word that people still whispered.

Tragically, my mother died nine months later. That was the beginning of my self-development in terms of women's health, because it impacted my life in such a severe and catastrophic way.

I felt deeply frustrated that I was hearing the same story over and over again: so many women were ignoring symptoms of female cancers, because they didn't really know their bodies. I felt this urge to create a campaign to try and help women get diagnosed earlier.

Then amazingly, my neighbour got a job as Head of Oncology for Gynaecological Cancers at the Royal Marsden hospital. One day she asked if I would help her to fundraise. I asked the hospital if we did this fundraising for them, could we also campaign about early diagnosis and prevention? And they agreed.

We started off with two separate projects: the *Gynaecological Cancer Fund*, which was for fundraising and then in 2015 we launched the *Lady Garden Campaign*. Eventually they merged

and became the Lady Garden Foundation, which is what we are today.

The main aim is to save women's lives. We want to make much better treatments available, specifically for the four gynaecological cancers. And we want to make as much noise as possible about women's bodies, so they know when something's not right.

I created a wonderful project in the Lady Garden Foundation, but I wanted to do something even more creative. I was working as an actress and a filmmaker, and wondered how I could use myself as a vessel to help get rid of the stigma attached to women's bodies, something outside of the cancer space.

I created *The Happy Vagina podcast*: a rapidly growing, international platform about real women. We talk about everything to do with women's bodies and empowerment across the spectrum.

Mika's object

I have a tiny antique box with Mary on it, and inside are my grandmother's rosary beads. When my grandmother passed away she left it to my mother. They were both immigrants, and they were both nurses. Everything I have today is because of the work they did to make the world a better place for women. It also represents my belief in something greater than me. I try to live each day with an awareness that as God's children, we have a responsibility to treat each other with respect and kindness.

SARAH STOREY

Dame Sarah Storey is a British Paralympian cyclist and swimmer who was born with a limb abnormality affecting the growth and function of her left hand. As a swimmer, she competed in four Paralympic Games – Barcelona 1992, Atlanta 1996, Sydney 2000 and Athens 2004 – and won five gold, eight silver, and three bronze medals. In 2005, she switched to track and road cycling and took two gold medals in Beijing 2008, four in London 2012 and three in Rio 2016, making her the most successful female British Paralympian of all time. She is a 40-time World Champion and has broken 76 world records, and also triumphed in non-disabled events, becoming the British National Track Champion six times. In 2012 and 2016 she was shortlisted for the *BBC Sports Personality of the Year*.

I grew up in the Peak District, the eldest of three. My left hand was never an emotional subject. My parents said, *'If there's anything you can't do, we'll help you find a way.'*

At primary school I was just like any other child. I was always sporty and, when I was eight, I won the trophy for being the fastest swimmer in the school. When I was six I saw the 1984 Olympics on TV and watched a 15-year-old called Sarah Hardcastle win medals. I wanted to be like her and worked out that I could go to the 1992 Games.

> *Within sport there is too much focus on the way we look.*

My swimming coach gave me the details of a lady to write to. She replied, inviting me to a swimming competition where I learnt about the Paralympics. I was then asked to a trial weekend in Birmingham. I started in the slowest lane, finished in the top lane and was challenging the boys to go faster. I was invited to compete in the Paralympic Games in Barcelona where I won two gold medals. I was 14. I have always had this intense drive to be the best I can, and that comes from something my parents said to me when I was a little girl: focus on what you are doing, on what you can control, and the beating of other people will come after that.

The Paralympics ran into the first term of Year 10 and I was bullied at school. It affected my confidence and I slid into the habit of not eating properly. It wasn't a conscious decision: controlling my eating was a way of trying to regain some of the control I felt I'd lost, and there was also pressure to portray a particular outward image.

Within sport there is too much focus on the way we look, and we have to call out the media and ask them to think, *'Would I write this about a male athlete?'* It's not about size or shape; and if you choose to wear make-up, that's your choice, it shouldn't be a requirement. The media has a role to play in making sure we talk about performance rather than image.

I'd always wanted to be a mum and, after the Games in London, I decided that I'd done everything I wanted to as an athlete, so if I couldn't come back to international sport it wouldn't matter. But, nine months after Louisa arrived, I was breaking a world record again!

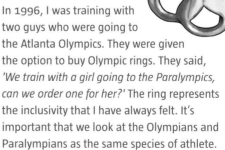

Sarah's object
In 1996, I was training with two guys who were going to the Atlanta Olympics. They were given the option to buy Olympic rings. They said, *'We train with a girl going to the Paralympics, can we order one for her?'* The ring represents the inclusivity that I have always felt. It's important that we look at the Olympians and Paralympians as the same species of athlete.

SONIA GUIMARÃES
Photography by Jessica Mangaba

*If you are diverse,
in gender, race, you
will only have better
results. Give everybody
an opportunity.*

SONIA GUIMARÃES

In 1989 Sonia Guimarães became the first black woman in Brazil to earn a doctorate in physics. She was the first black woman to teach at the Aeronautics Institute of Technology (ITA - Instituto Tecnológico de Aeronáutica) and the first woman to teach in the ITA's physics department where she is a professor of Physics. In 1976, Guimarães joined the Federal University of São Carlos becoming the first member of her family to attend University. She then moved to Italy to join the University of Bologna, then the University of Manchester Institute of Science and Technology in the United Kingdom. Alongside her academic work Guimarães has worked to improve diversity in Brazilian research, particularly the representation of black women in science and academia. She has given a series of academic lectures about her experiences of racism in academia and the impact of affirmative action programmes. In 2017 she was awarded the *Black Race Trophy* in recognition of her advocacy work.

I was born in São Paulo in the south-east of Brazil. My grandparents, my mother and my father did not have much formal education and so my mother found me a teacher, Miss Hilda, who was retired, but taught some kids at her house. I joined her home school and learned how to read and write. My mum bought me an Encyclopedia. And she said: *'Now, you get to read. Go find the answers for yourself.'*

When she is a little girl, and starts to want to play with cars, with Lego, or to open up your computer or phone to see what's inside, don't tell her these things are for boys. She may be an engineer in the future.

I grew up with my father, my mother and my three siblings. Two boys and two girls in total. When I was thirteen years old, my dad was diagnosed with tuberculosis and he had to be isolated. My mother is my inspiration, she never gave up. A neighbour was having a wedding and the caterer left her high and dry so my mother baked some pastries to sell. Then they asked her to cater a party. They needed a thousand of this, a thousand of that. Do you think my mother told them: *'I can't do that much'*? No way! She baked a huge cake, thousands of snacks. Fifty years later she is still catering for weddings of people whose parents she catered for. And people still remember her. So, she is my inspiration. I am her daughter and the apple doesn't fall far from the tree.

During high school, I took a Buildings course and when I graduated, I said to myself: *'Well, I have a Buildings degree, so I want to graduate in Construction Engineering'*. I started studying for the Engineering exam. Because I studied science, the teacher told me to choose between engineering courses. There were sixteen options. Thirteen were engineering. I chose all of them and the last three options were Physics. I fell in love with Physics. And I fell in love with semiconductors and now I have a PhD in semiconductors. Getting my PhD made me the first black Brazilian woman to get a PhD in Physics. I was the first woman and the first black woman to ever teach Physics on ITA.

I went to the Space and Aeronautics Institute, where I became the project manager for infrared radiation sensors. I even got a patent application, so I am a scientist and almost an inventor. I was supposed to have retired two years ago, but in 2019 *ITA* started having racial quotas and I wanted to stay to teach the black kids that would join. That year, 17 girls joined us. We never had so many girls!

Gender and racial diversity brings out new ideas, different ideas. You put a bunch of white men together talking about the same thing, and the result will be the same. Diversity brings profits; you consider more possibilities, you comprehend more people and you will understand more customers. If you are diverse, in gender and race, you will only have better results. Give everybody an opportunity.

Diversity brings profits; you consider more possibilities, you comprehend more people and you will understand more customers. If you are diverse, in gender and race, you will only have better results. Give everybody an opportunity.

I am a part of many groups trying to bring girls into science and these groups are all over the world. And how do we incentivise girls? When she is a little girl, and starts to want to play with cars, with Lego, or to open up your computer or phone to see what's inside, don't yell at her and don't tell her these things are for boys. Let her play with a toy truck and see if she likes it. She will try to disassemble this toy, she may be an engineer in the future. If you are a girl and your parents do not want you to go to science – you will slowly lose interest. So the girls come to us, fantastically breaking stereotypes and then they go on to produce great, genius work. So it must be reassessed, the barriers must be removed and the opportunities must be given to these girls.

I didn't know anybody in STEM, let alone a black female physicist. All my professors were men. I didn't have good female examples.

Now I am passing the torch. It's time for these kids to come up with ideas and to stand out, be successful, and be independent. My advice would be that it is possible, you can do it.

Sonia's object
My object is the *Raça Negra Award*. The NGO Afrobras created an award, the *Raça Negra Award*, to celebrate all the black people who are successful despite structural racism. I won the award just for being me; they didn't even know I was the first black doctor of Physics in Brazil. It was a beautiful celebration at the Teatro Municipal full of black people. My mom and I arrived in a limousine. I had never ridden in a limousine before. When Brazil celebrated 500 years from its discovery, we had a year full of parties. But no one remembered the Africans that were kidnapped, taken from their homes and brought here against their will. There was no tribute. The award was a beautiful thing and exposed me to so many more people. Because I won the award I also joined Afrobras, becoming their official translator and all of these things got me recognition and now lots of people know who I am. Once I did a talk in a small town which I'd never been to and a girl there came up to me and hugged me and cried saying *'I will study physics, because of you'*.

147

TARANA BURKE
Photography by Dougal MacArthur

As a community, we are collectively responsible for the safety of every person.

TARANA BURKE

Tarana Burke is an activist and the founder of the *Me Too* movement. She studied at university in Alabama, and worked in black arts and culture before starting Just Be, a non-profit organisation dedicated to the wellbeing of black teenage girls. In 2006, she began *Me Too*, which provided the survivors of sexual violence with support and pathways to healing. In 2017, women began to use the hashtag *#MeToo* to tweet about the Harvey Weinstein sexual abuse allegations. *#MeToo* went viral and became a global movement. Tarana was named 2017 *Time Person of the Year*. In 2020 she created *Act Too*, a digital platform that enables anyone, anywhere, to become active in the fight to end sexual violence. She has written a memoir called *Unbound*.

I grew up in the Bronx, New York, one of five girls. Our family is southern and Caribbean and politically conscious; I grew up immersed in black culture. I got good grades and loved to read. I was in the talented and gifted programme; I was an athlete and loved to dance.

In high school I was radical, at 14 I started organising and leading protests, fighting back against some of the racism at my school. I could identify injustice when I saw it, but I didn't have any tools to do anything about it. So, I joined a group connected to the 21st Century Youth Leadership Movement in Alabama, which developed young people into grassroots community organisers.

My dream was to be a track star and go to the Olympics, then I set out to be a teacher. I also wanted to be a writer. I didn't make the connection that I could be a writer and make a living so, when I got to college, I tried the teaching route. I took a course and, when I realised that wasn't going to work, thought about becoming a lawyer. But really, I wanted to be an organiser.

I was a survivor of sexual violence but I didn't talk about it. In 1996, at a youth camp, a 13-year-old girl revealed to me that she had been dealing with sexual violence. I was in my twenties and very new to the idea of being a survivor. I was grappling with my own stuff so, when she poured her heart out, I couldn't hear the story and, as a result, I couldn't help her.

I disappointed her and, when I started picking apart what had happened, I realised that all I really wanted to say to her was, *'I know exactly how you are feeling – this happened to me too.'*

I didn't start *Me Too* officially until 10 years later, but I started to work with girls straight away. I focused on black and brown girls. I was in a community that was grappling with a lot of sexual violence. This teacher or that coach would be arrested for messing with girls. My initial thought was: if I helped build their sense of self-worth and leadership skills, it would help them combat whatever they were feeling as a survivor. We kept having these incidents and I felt people responded as if it was the individual's problem – that girl was molested and needs to get therapy and that teacher needs to be fired and we've solved the problem – as opposed to wrapping our minds around the idea that, as a community, we are collectively responsible for the safety of every person.

Our response to sexual violence should look like our response to gun violence or police violence. We should be organising, we should be coming together to understand the roots of the problem, we should be looking at prevention and healing. I'd spent most of my life feeling like I was a particular kind of girl and that's why these things happened to me, so I was steeped in shame. As soon as I connected to others who understood deeply what I had experienced, whether they were survivors or just had the ability to empathise, the layers of shame started to peel away. I knew that there was power in empathy and that whatever work I did had to be driven by that. The idea of empowerment through empathy came before the name *Me Too* because empathy is what changed my life.

If you can teach little kids basic things like not to run with scissors and to say please and thank you, you can teach them boundaries and respect and consent.

We need to take steps to disrupt rape culture, which creates the space for violence to happen. The steps are tangible: in America 20 years ago, we smoked cigarettes everywhere and that's not the case now. It took multiple interventions: we had community intervention where people organised to get cigarette machines out of schools and public areas, and medical intervention with research about what tobacco does to your body and the dangers of second-hand smoke. It took years of organising and strategising to get to the point where, when a person pulls out a cigarette, we're like, *'Ooh, you're trying to kill us!'*

The same can happen with sexual violence if we collectively decide to intervene. We need cultural, political, medical and narrative interventions and we all need to work in tandem. That's why we created an addendum to *Me Too* called *Act Too*, because everybody has a role to play. If we stopped showing egregious sexual violence on television and in movies that would be a massive shift. We need research interventions showing the cost of sexual violence – the money lost in wages and medical bills; the long-term effects of PTSD on a person.

Comprehensive sex education is also needed. If you can teach little kids basic things like not to run with scissors and to say please and

thank you, you can teach them boundaries and respect and consent. Teach that from kindergarten to high school and, when young people who will have been immersed in these ideas since they were children go to college, you will reduce sexual violence on campuses. All this can work.

We need men to feel they have space in this movement. There are men who are survivors, there are men who are allies and advocates, and we need to hear more of their voices so people don't see this as a gendered situation. We need the trans community, the gender fluid; we need everybody because everybody is affected.

Tarana's object
There is a tradition in Caribbean families to wear bangles. I have bracelets from my mother: one was given to her by my grandfather, another she gave me when I had my daughter. I was given a set when I finished high school, another set when I finished college. My jewellery reminds me of the strength of my family and my ancestors, the people whose shoulders I stand on. My mother is the epitome of strength and perseverance and resilience and sacrifice. I always want to be reminded of that. She exposed me to the things that helped me to be who I am, and these objects that I wear keep me close to my mom.

LA ROUX

Elly Jackson is a singer, songwriter and producer. She wrote songs with Ben Langmaid while she was still at school and they went on to become La Roux, releasing an eponymous album in 2009. They had hits with *In For The Kill* and *Bulletproof* and won a Grammy award for best electronic/dance album. La Roux had a second UK top ten album with *Trouble in Paradise* in 2014. After Jackson and Langmaid parted company, she retained the name La Roux as her stage persona and in 2020, she released *Supervision* under her own label, Supercolour Records.

My dad taught me to play the guitar: I saw him playing and thought it was the coolest thing. I didn't want to be a girl with a guitar, I wanted to be Jimi Hendrix or Buddy Holly. I was inspired by Joni Mitchell, Carole King and Annie Lennox but I never felt that I could be one of those women. I had no problems saying I was a girl and being a girl, but I've always wanted to be boys.

At school I was a nightmare. I didn't know that I had bad dyslexia and ADD. I only found out I had ADD recently which, in hindsight, explains a lot of my behaviour. I felt very misunderstood. I just wanted to play music and dance. I felt that school was a complete waste of my time because I already knew exactly what I wanted to do with my life.

I met Ben when I was 17, we spent two or three years getting to know each other, meeting up once or twice a week to write songs. The release of *In For The Kill* was when I realised that La Roux was going to be much more than I ever imagined. The single stayed at number two in the charts for weeks. Winning the Grammy was a big deal, but awards ceremonies don't really mean anything. A better reward is to feel good about your work as a creative person, and the best thing is seeing people singing along to something that you wrote.

My handling of success was not good at all. I don't think I realised the dream came with so much pressure. The lack of anonymity overnight freaked me out. I got chased down the road by paparazzi and once I remember being on the floor of a car, crying to my mum on the phone – that's how much I didn't like it.

When you are someone who can generate money for a company, you are expected to keep performing. There were millions of suggestions every day. Why don't you wear a little bit more make up? Have you ever thought of wearing something a bit more figure-hugging? All that stuff made me feel insanely uncomfortable. They tried to manufacture me and it made me really nervy. I felt judged by everyone all the time. Obviously, it is very different now: being androgynous or non-binary is not something that anyone would argue with any more. Now I am in my thirties, I feel more at ease with myself, with my sexuality, with my confidence. I know what I want for my career. My aim is to continue to produce for the rest of my life and for other women to see me doing that job.

Elly's object

I bought a porcelain elephant right at the end of a bad working relationship. My sister gave me an elephant when I was born, because I am called Elly. I saw this elephant online and thought, *'That's mine.'* It reminds me of when I was eight and I had my own way of dressing. Up to the early days of La Roux, I dressed like that. Then, suddenly, I was in outfits that were nothing like me. The elephant represents the fact that I am now doing it my way.

MARGARET CHO

Margaret Cho is a comedian, actor, musician, entrepreneur and activist. Born in San Francisco to Korean immigrant parents, she started her stand-up career at the age of 14 and after winning a competition to open for Jerry Seinfeld in the early 1990s. She has starred in her own sitcoms - *All American Girl*, *The Cho Show* and toured extensively with her one-woman shows – most recently *Fresh off the Bloat* – as well as featuring in (among others) *30 Rock*, *Good on Paper*, *Dancing with the Stars*, *Law and Order The Masked Singer*, and *High Maintenance*. In 2020, she appeared in three films, including as Auntie Ling in Netflix's Academy Award nominated animation, *Over the Moon*. She has a podcast, *The Margaret Cho*. A five-times Grammy and Emmy Award nominee, she is also an anti-racism, anti-bullying and gay rights activist.

My family emigrated to the United States in 1964, and in 1976, my father bought a gay bookstore. My parents' bookstore was downstairs from a pub that had a comedy night. I would work at the bookstore and, when I finished, I would go upstairs and do comedy. A theatre teacher at my school signed me up for open mic nights and that made all the difference because when you're supported by other women you feel that you're not alone.

I was very shy at school, there was racial discrimination plus, it was a very homophobic time in a very homophobic city. I was having to confront graffiti with my name in it saying I was a lesbian – well, now I'm like, *'duh, of course!'* – but when you're 10, it's really scary. As adults we come to understand and accept our identity – and it's great – but as a child you just want to fit in.

There are such crazy beauty standards for Koreans. I was always told I was too fat, too loud, too big, too whatever. You internalise all that and you minimise all the things that make you spectacular. But it did mean that when I was starting out I felt I had nothing to lose. On stage I feel safe. It's exhilarating to make people laugh. And laughter gives you hope.

I've always been ambitious. People cast female ambition in a negative light because they want to hold us back. It's misogynistic. By improving your station in life, you set things up for other women to improve their lives.

Laughter gives you hope.

Joan Rivers, my friend and mentor, was hugely supportive and reassuring about my future, my funniness, my talents. She died in 2014 and I miss her very much. I took over her spot on the show *Fashion Police*, on the red carpet, which was a really great honour. The best advice she ever gave me, was that if you're a comedian, they're always going to want you. Funny women are sought after, and the older you get, the more you're needed.

Margaret's object
My object is a *thangka* (a Tibetan scroll painting) that hangs on my wall. There was a general strike in Kathmandu the day I bought it, and the Tibetan royal family was assassinated on the same day – which was also the day I was leaving Tibet. The airport was mayhem and I was smuggling it out because you can't buy these things and it's illegal to take them out of the country. I will never smuggle anything again, but the thangka reminds me that I have gone from a shy kid who was scared of everything to being an international art smuggler!

155

EMMA DABIRI

It didn't make sense being black and Irish; there weren't other people like that in my life.

EMMA DABIRI

Emma Dabiri is a presenter, social historian and writer. Emma's interdisciplinary work crosses African Studies, art, sociology, history, film, literature, theatre and music. She is a teaching fellow in the Africa department at SOAS. In 2019 she published her first book *Don't Touch My Hair*; her second, *What White People Can Do Next: From Allyship to Coalition*, followed in 2021 and was an instant bestseller. Emma has made documentaries for Channel 4 and BBC4 and co-presents Britain's *Lost Masterpieces* on BBC 4 and *Virtually History* on YouTube Originals. She was on the judging panel for the 2020-21 *Merky Books New Writers Prize* which was founded by Stormzy to discover unpublished, under-represented young writers from the UK and Ireland.

I was born in Dublin, Ireland and, soon after, we moved to the American south. My mum is Irish, my dad Nigerian and a lot of his family had moved to Atlanta, Georgia. We lived in a big house and extended family – grandparents, cousins and uncles and aunts – were always staying. After four years, we moved back to Dublin where I spent the rest of my childhood and teens.

I went to lots of different schools, I didn't stay at any for very long. I think on a fundamental and subconscious level I was quite resistant to the system: it felt like there were a lot of pointless rules. I also experienced racism. I was one of the only black children in most of my schools, and attitudes towards black people were such that I would be punished disproportionately for quite minor indiscretions.

I often found it difficult to concentrate and to engage. I did an IQ test when I was eight and, because of the results, it was suggested that I move up a year because I wasn't being challenged enough. The school responded badly; they didn't think I should be rewarded for not concentrating. So that didn't happen.

At that time, the notions that people in Ireland had about black people were often quite one dimensional. There was this dynamic of white saviourism where Irish missionaries would go and help poor, starving Africans. There was an attitude that I should be grateful that I was in

Ireland and not some famine-ridden, war-torn country. At school we used to collect pennies for the starving black babies in Africa, and I remember going on holiday to Nigeria and seeing skyscrapers and quite a lot of wealth in Lagos. Obviously, it was only in certain sections of society, but it was more wealth than I'd seen in 1980s Ireland. I came back and said, *'I don't think they need our charity.'* I got hauled out of the class and my teacher said, *'You need to stop making up stories.'*

I didn't just grow up in a homogenously white area, I grew up in a homogenously white country. It didn't make sense being black and Irish; there weren't other people like that in my life. I remember my mum saying to me, *'You have a unique perspective; it's like a USP.'* And I was like, *'Whatever. I wish I was American.'*

Me being Irish was something that was challenged regularly – the expectation was that I was from elsewhere. Sometimes people in the U.K. say, *'You are really in touch with your Irish side.'* I'm like what do you mean? I am from Ireland. Being Irish, and having been born and raised in Dublin, is a defining part of me, not in a nationalistic sense but in terms of cultural frequencies. Culturally, I feel very much a product of Dublin specifically, and Ireland more broadly. I would say my sensibilities, my humour and my outlook are very Irish.

I was an avid reader from a young age and I read a lot of black American literature. I felt alienated and reading was a refuge, those writers a lifeline. While I consumed books, I never imagined that I would write myself. I think younger me would be really excited that I have written books that are in the black canon.

Through the politicisation of black hair, we can tell a lot about society at any given time.

With *Don't Touch My Hair* I wanted to put paid to the idea that, when we talk about black hair, it's something shallow and superficial. Hair is of great significance to African cultures and I wanted to look at both the physical and metaphysical aspects. Through the politicisation of black hair, we can tell a lot about society at any given time. So, in many ways, it's a history book: it goes right back to the 1500s and pre-colonial Africa, before there is any stigma attached to black hair. The stigma first emerges in the processes of racialisation that happen as a result of the transatlantic slave trade.

With *What White People Can Do Next*, I explain the way in which the idea of a white race was invented. We can trace it back to an actual year: 1661 is the first time we see the idea of a white race being spoken about in a set of laws in colonial Barbados, drawn up after uprisings by indentured Irish labourers and enslaved Africans who came together to fight the English, and sometimes Scottish landlords, who exploited their labour. The invention of race shut down solidarities that were threatening to the power system.

From its inception, the idea of whiteness is constructed around the notion of an inherent superiority, and the idea of blackness is constructed around the notion of an inherent inferiority, which serves to justify the enslavement of the people who become known as black. We will never achieve the resolutions that we hope to unless we understand that race is a social construct.

Social media has a lot of power and possibility for change, but it is the quintessential poisoned chalice. The nature of some platforms, particularly Twitter, has gamified division. Because of the word count, people deal with complicated ideas in a very reductive way. Social media rewards outrage so you amass more likes, more retweets, more followers and more influence. Concepts are untethered from the environments in which they were generated and used in distorted ways and that is a recipe for disaster.

We live in a system that is predicated on inequality so, if one group gets their seat at the table, it's going to be at the expense of somebody else. I would like to see a world in which economic growth and the pursuit of profit is not the principal aim, and the creation of societies where resources are distributed equally, and the earth is respected and not exploited.

Emma's object

I have a teddy bear that was given to me by my Nigerian grandmother when I was six months old. When you see pictures of me as toddler, I always have this small brown bear and I still have it now. Its face has kind of dissolved, it only has eyes left. It's mechanical, you wind it up and it plays a lullaby. Growing up I had quite an unstable life in many ways: I've moved lots of times and gone to different schools but I've always had that teddy bear. It feels like a constant in a life of change, and now I've given it to my elder son.

KATHRINE SWITZER

Kathrine Switzer is an athlete, sports and social advocate, author, and Emmy award-winning television commentator. In 1967 she became the first woman to officially run the Boston Marathon and, in 1974, she won the New York City Marathon. She created the Avon International Running Circuit of women-only races in 27 countries which led to the inclusion of a women's marathon in the Olympics for the first time, in the 1984 Games. She is a journalist and founder of the global non-profit, 261 Fearless, which aims to empower and unite women through running.

When I was 12, I wanted to be pretty and popular at high school and I thought the passport to that was to become a cheerleader. My dad said, *'You want people to cheer for you. The game is on the field. Life is to participate not spectate. If you run a mile a day from now until autumn, you could be the best player on the high school field hockey team.'* As I went for my first jog, he said, *'It's not about going fast, it's about finishing the job.'* That pearl of wisdom changed my life.

My friends said, *'Running will give you big legs and chest hair; nobody's going to date you, it's not cool to sweat.'* And they would whisper, *'You probably won't be able to have kids; your uterus is going to fall out.'* I ignored the myths.

I went on to study journalism at Syracuse University, a powerhouse for men's sports. There were no women's sports. I asked the coach of the men's cross-country team if I could train with them. He said, *'You can't be on the team, that's against the rules, but you can work out with us and we would welcome you.'* But, as I left his office, he laughed, *'I got rid of her!'* The next day I showed up.

When I was with the cross-country team, Arnie, the university mailman and a volunteer coach, regaled me with stories about the Boston Marathon – he'd run 15 times. I said, *'We should do it.'*

On the entry form there was nothing about gender. Arnie said, *'Of course not, they wouldn't think a woman would want to run.'*

I signed my name, K V Switzer - the officials had no idea and issued me with the number 261.

The race began and the journalists were excited to see me and took pictures. Suddenly, I heard, *'Get the hell out of my race!'* He tried to rip the 261 off my chest and off my back, ripping the corner. The official smacked Arnie away and came after me. I was terrified and humiliated. It was an ugly incident and I felt like going home. Then I realised that's what everyone expected me to do. I said to Arnie, *'I am going to finish the race on my hands and knees if I have to.'*

I started the race as a girl and finished as a woman. By the time I crossed the finish line, I knew I wanted two things: to become a better athlete and to create opportunities for women in sports.

Kathrine's object
I look at my number from the Boston Marathon every day. It became a magic number: people sent pictures of themselves racing with 261 on their backs, or even tattooed on their arms. It dawned on me that women had been given the realisation that they could do anything, and they felt fearless. So, I formed 261 Fearless, a non-profit that encourages people to run. Running has given me everything – my career, my friends, fitness, travel and my husband – but most of all, it's given me myself.

Photography by Hagen Hopkins

LESLEE UDWIN

Leslee Udwin, formerly a filmmaker, is now a human rights campaigner. She won the 2015 *Anna Lindh Prize* for human rights activism and the 2019 *UN Women for Peace Activism in Arts and Education Award*. Her awards as a producer and director include a BAFTA and her films include *Who Bombed Birmingham?* (1990), about the Birmingham Six, who were subsequently released after 17 years of wrongful imprisonment; and *India's Daughter* (2015), about the rape and murder of Jyoti Singh. She founded the Think Equal non-profit charity in 2016.

My father wanted me to be a lawyer, as he was. He was adamant that I was wasting my brain, my life, in pursuing a career in acting. I was made even more determined and I learned to be resilient. I became a producer, having left acting, in order to be in charge of the story, and I played myself in a BBC film based on that true story.

India's Daughter **was a** huge turning point in my life. I'd been raped at 18. I imagined that I'd be furious sitting opposite the rapists that I was determined to interview. I knew that if I didn't look into the eyes of the men that did this to that young girl – the most brutal, unimaginable cruelty, quite apart from the rape – and find out what kind of human beings they were, then I wouldn't make that film. Because we need to know how to change, not just be reactive to the horrific abuses of human rights that are ubiquitous in the world.

Only one of the men I interviewed in those prison cells had finished secondary school. Two weeks later I was interviewing their legal team who, despite having had the highest degree of access to what we call education, were worse than the rapists. They made the rapists sound like normal, ordinary men. That is when I understood that, while education is the only way we can change mindsets, it's not mere access to education, and certainly not the kind of education we currently give our children. That system is broken and not fit for purpose.

Research yielded the fact that the human brain is 90% developed by the age of five. If we want to put in a foundation of values,

empathy, moral compass, character, self-regulation, emotional literacy, gender equality, peaceful conflict resolution, we've got to do it before the age of six.

I realised there was something much bigger than me and my ambitions for my career.

That is why I founded the *Think Equal NGO*. It's a very concrete programme that is teachable by anyone. I resolved to give the rest of my life to ensuring that every child in every classroom, in every country, gets a foundation in the competencies and skills that child needs to have positive outcomes in life. We are in 16 countries, with 129,000 children across six continents, to date. We have a lot of journeys still to make – it's a big world out there.

Leslee's object
My husband and I were in Prague, browsing in this charming old shop, and we came across a beautiful antique ceramic statue of a woman, looking down into ample skirts where the sculptor has created fields and animals, and people and children. To me, it represents all the nurturing, loving and caring female values that will change the world when women are allowed to express them in leadership.

BERNARDINE EVARISTO
Photography by Suki Dhanda

When you think about where you want to be in five years' time, don't come up with a realistic answer, come up with an unrealistic vision.

BERNARDINE EVARISTO

Bernardine Evaristo is the author of eight books and numerous other works of verse fiction, short stories, poetry, essays, literary criticism, journalism and drama. In 2019 she was the first black woman, and the first black British person, to win the *Booker Prize* with her novel *Girl, Woman, Other*, which was top of the Sunday Times bestseller list for five weeks and in the top 10 for 44 weeks. She received an OBE in 2020 and was voted one of 100 *Great Black Britons* in 2021. She is Professor of Creative Writing at Brunel University London; an Honorary Fellow at St. Anne's College, Oxford University, a Vice President of the Royal Society of Literature and President of Rose Bruford College of Theatre and Performance. Her first non–fiction book is *Manifesto: On Never Giving Up* (October 2021).

I didn't suffer a lot of in-your-face racism when I was a child but as a family we did. Kids used to smash our windows all the time. A neighbour let his dog foul our garden and when my dad asked him what he was doing, he called my dad a *'black bastard'* and started a fight then followed him into the house. That was what you lived with.

I grew up in Woolwich, on the River Thames in south-east London. It was a very white area, and we were the only black family for a long time. My father didn't pass on his culture to us. He spoke Yoruba but not to us. It was a very British childhood, but you felt your difference. People were disapproving. My mother was a white woman with loads of mixed-race children gathered around her. There was a level of hostility without it being directly confrontational.

Books can create a very deep connection to other people's lives and cultures.

There were eight of us, four boys and four girls. My mother was Roman Catholic and didn't use contraception. My father had come to Britain from Nigeria in 1949 and my mother was white English, but on both sides of my family history there was interracial and intercultural mixing, so it's not as simple as English and Nigerian. She faced huge resistance from her family when she decided to marry a black man. But she loved him, and they were together for 33 years: it's a long time for a mixed marriage of that time.

My father was a welder in a factory. My mother was a teacher, but she had eight children in 10 years and didn't go back to teaching until the last one went to school; we were very poor. We couldn't go on holiday. We shared a bicycle between eight children. My father wasn't so good at being a dad because he didn't talk to us and he was too disciplinarian. But he joined the Labour party and became a political activist and I love that about him. That was how he dealt with prejudice: he became a fighter against it. Both my parents fought for equality. They are the source of my politics and that's what's kept me writing all these years. I wanted to write about black British lives.

We were called half-caste in the sixties and seventies. These racial terms change. *'Coloured'* is in, then it's out, and *'black'* is in, and *'of colour'* is kind of acceptable, and then BAME is in, but now seems like it's on its way out. Eventually, people objected to half-caste. You're not half of something. And so mixed race and biracial became the terms.

I was quite integrated in my community, to be honest, even though I was seen as different. I went to a grammar school. You had to pass the eleven-plus to get in and there was a high expectation of academic achievement. At the

DR JASVINDER SANGHERA

This concept, honour, is invested in how you behave. And if your parents say this to you from a young age it becomes normal. Asserting yourself means you don't love your family. But, actually, it's about property and control.

DR JASVINDER SANGHERA

Jasvinder Sanghera is the founder of Karma Nirvana, a charity that supports women and men affected by forced marriages and honour-based abuse. Born in Derby in 1965, she ran away from home at the age of 16 rather than marry a man she had never met. She founded Karma Nirvana following the suicide of her sister Robina. Jasvinder Sanghera's work is recognised as a contributory factor in the creation of a specific UK forced-marriage criminal offence in 2014. She was made a CBE in 2013 in recognition of her services to victims of forced marriage and honour-based violence.

I am one of seven sisters, one younger than me, all the rest older. As children, we shared a bed. It was a very small house. We played together. We pulled each other's hair. It was a good childhood. It was only as we got older that I started seeing my sisters being taken out of school at the age of 15 to be married.

Robina was two years older than me, Yasmin four years older. I saw them disappear and come back as someone's wife and I realised I couldn't have thoughts of freedom or independence, couldn't think about education. I was being groomed to be somebody's wife. It became real when Robina disappeared. She was the one above me and she was away from school for nine months, and when she came back, she was put down into my year at school because she'd missed so much. And then I knew it was going to be my turn.

I was born in Britain. I'm as British as anybody. I don't know India, where my parents came from. What happened to my sisters happened 40 years ago – but I question why even then a nine-month absence from school wasn't of concern to anyone. And young girls are still going missing off our school rolls. Some people fear being called a racist if they intervene. They misguidedly think it's cultural. But this is a safeguarding issue. This is about taking away girls' rights to choose who they want to marry – and, equally, their rights to education. When it comes to abuse, I expect to be treated the same way as anyone else.

The sad fact about this kind of abuse is that women are often perpetrators. It was my mother who sat me down one day after school and presented me with this photograph of a man. I learned I had been promised to him since the age of eight. I remember looking at this photograph and thinking, *'He's shorter than me, he's older than me. And actually, I don't want to marry a stranger. You know, I'm 14."*

I was fearful of speaking out because I'd never seen anyone in my family stand up to my mother. But I said, *'I'm not marrying him, mum. I want to go to school, to university.'* My mother was very clear that there was no need for an education, and I would not dishonour the family and say no.

I kept protesting. My parents took me out of school, and I was held prisoner until I agreed to the marriage. I was locked in a room that was padlocked on the outside. I attempted to take my own life twice. They wouldn't take me to the hospital because they feared me telling someone there. In the end, I agreed to the marriage simply to escape.

I ran away from home at the age of 16. I went to Newcastle. I had no experience of life. I'd never been into town on my own. I was missing my family terribly. My parents reported me missing to the police and I called home and said, *'Please let me come back. But I won't marry that man.'* And my mother was very clear that either I come home and marry him; or, she said, *'You are dead in our eyes and we will never speak of you again.'*

I have been disowned by my family for 47 years, as have my three children and three

170

grandchildren. I love my parents dearly. If they had stood up to the community, the community would have disowned them. Under the so-called honour system, a woman's sexuality is controlled by the family. This concept, honour, is invested in how you behave. And if your parents say this to you from a young age it becomes normal. Asserting yourself means you don't love your family. But, actually, it's about property and control.

Under the so-called honour system, a woman's sexuality is controlled by the family.

When my father died, he made me executor of his will. He spoke a thousand words in death. I remember going back to the house for the first time, walking upstairs and there on the wall was my graduation picture. I had invited him to my graduation, but he wouldn't come.

My sister Robina had a secret relationship with me from when I was 18 and she talked my mother into seeing me. When my daughter Natasha was born, she brought my mother to the hospital. She refused to look at me, but she was there. Robina's marriage was horrific. She told the family and they encouraged her to go back. She took her own life. And still the family felt that was the honourable thing to do.

Karma Nirvana was founded as a result of Robina's suicide. I wanted people to hear about forced marriages. The helpline started in my front room and then the government funded it in 2008 and it has received over 180,000 calls for support. In 2021 we're dealing with over 900 calls a month. The call handlers are trained in risk assessment. They're not going to be sceptical or say, *'Isn't that part of your culture?'* We get calls from men and women, and from many young people. Our campaigning has increased awareness. The police, schools, GP practices, and social workers are now less likely to look away. After Robina died, my mother became very ill. I would go and see her at the

house in secret. Even at the hospice, the day she was dying, she told me to leave before the family arrived. But I refused to go — and then they walked in, my brother, my sisters. They were all round the bed, giving me dirty looks, which is fine, and my mother passed away, quietly, and I heard her dying words in Punjabi: *'Robina, I'm coming to you.'* She knew that Robina's death was wrong, but she couldn't say it out loud in a family, a community that wouldn't have accepted her.

My daughter Natasha married an Indian boy. I'll be honest, when she was growing up, I said, *'Whatever you do, don't marry an Indian boy.'* She said, *'You can't say that, mum, it's racist.'* So she goes off to uni, meets this Indian boy, and, to my shame, he was guilty until proven innocent. His grandparents came from the same part of Punjab as my parents, but his family didn't mind who he married as long as she was a Leeds United supporter. And we had this big fat Indian wedding. I have embraced the wonderful things about my heritage because I realise now that people are using that as an excuse to abuse. Not one of my family was there, but my daughter had that day because of the decision her mother made at 16: the right to choose.

Jasvinder's object
When I was disowned, my mother used to talk to me in secret. She had a ring made for me from Indian gold. I went with her to the jewellers in secret, and it was a moment of connection and love. I had a car accident and it had to be cut off my finger and it still has that cut in it. And I look at it and think that not everything that is broken has to be fixed. I'll live with the broken bits and that keeps me connected to her. And I will pass it on to my daughters and they will pass it on to theirs.

ELIZABETH NYAMAYARO
Photography by Behind The Cause

If you exist as part of a community, it's up to you to play your part in uplifting those around you.

ELIZABETH NYAMAYARO

Elizabeth Nyamayaro grew up in a small village in Zimbabwe and did not attend school until she was 10 years old. In her early twenties, she moved to London, where she studied politics at the London School of Economics and Political Science. She is currently United Nations Special Advisor for the *World Food Programme*, the world's largest humanitarian organisation working to end global hunger – and in her previous role as United Nations Senior Advisor on Gender Equality, she launched *HeForShe*, a global movement to encourage men and people of all genders to work for gender equality. Nyamayaro has worked at the forefront of global development for over two decades improving the lives of underserved populations and has held leadership roles at the World Bank, *World Health Organization*, UNAIDS, Merck and UN Women. In 2021, she published her memoir, *A Girl from Africa*.

I'm lucky enough to have known what I wanted to do from an early age, because of something that happened to me when I was eight years old. There we were, in a village in Zimbabwe, part of a small community, living off the land with an abundance of food. I was brought up by my gogo, my grandmother and it was a very lovely childhood. We all took care of each other.

But one year a severe drought hit. We went for days without food. I was so weak with hunger I was unable to move. I thought I was going to die. And then a miracle happened. This girl in a blue uniform found me and gave me a bowl of porridge. It saved my life. And I knew then that this was what I wanted to be. I wanted to be just like her, so that one day I could maybe save lives of others in a way that my life had been saved.

The norm in our village was that boys went to school and girls stayed at home. From the age of five, I was in charge of my grandmother's 11 goats. With the other young girls, I was in charge of fetching water, which took several hours a day.

At the age of 10, I went to Harare, to a British school. I couldn't speak, read or write English, the official language of the school. I was bullied for being an outsider. I think it was at this time that I realised how unequal the world could be. Because I was born a girl, I was far behind in my learning. There was the racial inequality because of the colour of my skin, and the social inequality because of my humble upbringing.

In my twenties, I decided I was going to chase my dream to work for the United Nations (UN). I landed at Heathrow Airport with a small suitcase and £250. Anything that could go wrong went wrong. I didn't know anyone in the UK. I ran out of money. I nearly became homeless. I worked as a janitor. Eventually I managed to put myself through university.

A person is only a person through other persons: we are all connected by our shared humanity.

My family is very proud that I didn't give up; but, in terms of the actual work, it's sort of expected. There's an African saying: *'To whom much is given, much is expected.'* Core to our African cultures is the ancient philosophy of *ubuntu*, the idea that a person is only a person through other persons: we are all connected by our shared humanity. What impacts one of us will eventually impact all of us in various ways. If you exist as part of a community, it's up to you to play your part in uplifting those around you.

In 2014, I found myself with the incredible opportunity, as United Nations Senior Advisor on Gender Equality, to figure out a way to uplift half of the world's population: women and girls. For a very long time, men and other genders have been excluded from this conversation. I immediately knew that we had to bring everyone together, including men. With the support of my colleagues, we created the *HeForShe* movement. Within three days, at least one man in every single country had joined; and within the first five days there were 1.2 billion online conversations.

HeForShe began to normalise the idea that gender inequality is society's issue, because when women gain, societies gain. *HeForShe* gave men an opportunity to examine their privilege and say, '*I will not rape a woman,*' rather than putting the burden on women not to get raped; '*I will not marry a child,*' rather than placing the burden on girls to escape child marriage. There was a lot of controversy over engaging men; a lot of pushback from some feminists who rightfully felt embittered by male oppression. But I think real change happens when we work as a collective, and, with regard to gender equality, no one is equal until we're all equal.

I owe so much to my gogo, my grandmother, who formed the core of who I am today. She taught me what it means to be African – which is to be blessed, but also to realise that you find your humanity by seeing it in others. It would be hard to find a more hardworking, dedicated and diligent person than my mother, who did everything to feed her family and to make sure that I and my three siblings went to school.

I also look up to my former boss at the United Nations, Phumzile Mlambo-Ngcuka, who worked alongside Nelson Mandela in the anti-apartheid movement and rose to become the first female Deputy President of South Africa in 2005. There is no way we would have been able to launch *HeForShe* if not for

her visionary leadership. I looked up to her when I was 11 and to find myself working with her was a dream come true.

I am comfortable being called ambitious. The thing I'm uncomfortable with is that I don't hear this question being asked of men. I have to remind myself sometimes, when I feel out of place – when you look around the room and there are 10 men and you're the only woman – that it didn't happen by fluke. It happened by hard work.

My advice is always to lift others as you rise. If you're a woman dealing with intersectional issues, the more you can have people like yourself alongside, the better. The more you normalise people like yourself as you climb, the easier it becomes for the next generation, and the easier it becomes for you. If there's one of you, it's a token, but if there's three, you start creating the norm around the table.

The UN said recently that we have lost two decades of progress towards the sustainable development goals because of the pandemic. We know there are at least 130 million girls out of school as a result; in moments of disaster, it's women and girls who are impacted the most. We have to place women at the centre of the recovery because the issue of gender inequality is really about power – right? – who has it, how they use it, and for whose benefit. The way we can rebuild better, post-Covid, is by making sure women are placed in positions of power.

Elizabeth's object

My object is this necklace of a map of Africa. It's a reminder of where I come from. I wear it every single day as a reminder that I am a child of African soil. I'm not always able to go home due to work, and having it so close says everything about my identity and my pride in knowing I am an African.

DR JULIE SMITH

Dr Julie Smith is a clinical psychologist & online educator who shares bite-sized mental health, pop psychology and motivational content online. After running her own private practice, she set out to reach a bigger, young audience by uploading both informative and engaging self-help videos. During the COVID-19 pandemic, Dr Julie's audience on TikTok grew astronomically as young people related to the videos she was making about mental health and put her advice to use. She now has millions of followers on TikTok.

I grew up in a small town in Hampshire, in the South of England. Neither of my parents had particularly privileged backgrounds and they both worked really hard to ensure that we had a secure, safe home to grow up in.

I always followed what I found most interesting; a degree in Psychology sounded interesting so I went with that. Even after university I still didn't know what I wanted to do. I found some jobs in research that sounded fascinating to me. It's been a meandering road towards being a psychologist and working in mental health.

As a young woman I didn't think about children; I wanted to completely focus on a career. The moment I had my daughter that changed completely and I realised then that nothing else would ever mean as much to me. So it became more about having a career around being a mum. I found it more difficult to move up in my profession; I wanted to work part time and it was difficult to do that, which is why I ended up working for myself.

I was working as a clinical psychologist and I noticed that a lot of the young people coming to me didn't really need long term therapy. A part of therapy is educational; you teach people about how the mind works, how to influence mood and manage emotions. A lot of people, once they had that information, were ready to go. They found it empowering and I kept talking to people about how it should be made available and should be free. People shouldn't have to see a therapist to find out simple life skills. So my husband and I decided to have a go and I started making a couple of YouTube videos. Then we found TikTok and tried to make some really short snappy videos and it took off. It turns out people were really hungry for that information.

I wish people knew that they had more influence over how they feel. People think that if they don't feel happy all the time, it's a weakness or something they're getting wrong, but actually it is a normal part of being human. There are lots of really simple ways we can influence how we feel. I want people to have information that is empowering to them to help them make life a bit easier.

Julie's object

The object I chose is a necklace that my mum bought for me. It has three little rings joined together and it has the names of my three children on it, it's just a lovely reminder of everything that matters to me. When you get into a whirlwind of lots of stuff happening in your career, it brings you back to what matters. While everything has been fantastic, it could all disappear tomorrow and I wouldn't mind because my family and the people around me are what matter most.

GEENA DAVIS

*We need to change
what kids see on-
screen. If it happens
on-screen, it will
happen in real life:
life will imitate art.*

GEENA DAVIS

Geena Davis is a multi-award winning actor and Founder of the non-profit Geena Davis Institute on Gender in Media. In 1989, Davis received the *Academy Award for Best Supporting Actress* for her role in Lawrence Kasdan's *The Accidental Tourist*. As an actor, Davis has appeared in several culturally historic roles, in particular her portrayal of Thelma in *Thelma and Louise,* for which she was nominated for an Oscar, and as the first female President of the USA in the 2006 TV series *Commander in Chief.* In 2004 she founded the Geena Davis Institute on Gender in Media, a non-profit research organisation that researches gender representation in media and advocates for equal representation of women. The institute is successfully influencing film and television content creators to dramatically increase the percentages of female characters and reduce gender stereotyping in media. Geena is an official partner of UN Women, working toward their goal of promoting gender equality and empowering women worldwide.

I grew up in Wareham, Massachusetts. My parents were both from Vermont, very old-fashioned New England. We heated our house with wood my father chopped. My mom grew all of our food. We were very underexposed to everything. My father worked on the Cape Cod Canal for the Army Corps of Engineers, and my mother was a teacher's assistant.

At school I was all gangly and awkward, and my dream was to take up less space in the world. The basketball team tried to recruit me because of my height, even though I told them I did not know how to play. They said to me, *'Well just stand there. You're the tallest girl in the country!'*

Growing up in Massachusetts, I was raised to be such a demure, polite child. So, it's been my life's work to become more authentic. It's kind of ambitious, but I really believe there are no limits on what we can do and learn no matter what age we are.

Seventeen years ago, while watching a preschool show with my then 2-year old daughter, I was stunned to see that there seemed to be far more male characters than female characters in something made specifically for the youngest kids. Then I saw it everywhere. As a mother, I thought, in the 21st century, why on earth would we be

showing kids from the beginning that boys are far more important than girls?

Media images are a powerful force in shaping perceptions of our value to society. When you see someone like yourself on screen, doing interesting and important things, you get the message: *'There's someone like me. I must matter.'* The stark gender inequality in media aimed at young children is significant, whether digital, television, movies or gaming, and wields enormous influence on kids who are developing a sense of their role and purpose in our society. And since children watch the same content repeatedly, negative stereotypes get imprinted again and again.

If the content we're making for them has a profound lack of unique and diverse female characters, boys and girls are unconsciously taking in the message that girls and women are not as valuable to our society as men and boys. This may inform their views throughout their lives. My theory of change is this: one of the easiest ways to immediately influence the stubborn issue of gender inequality, in all sectors of our society, is to change what they see on-screen first. If it happens on-screen, it will happen in real life: life will imitate art.

Why teach something from the beginning that's so hard to get rid of later? Just show kids from the beginning that boys and girls share the sandbox equally; that they are equally impressive, fun and essential, and they're each – by the way – half of the population.

In 2004 I launched the Geena Davis Institute on Gender in Media and sponsored the most extensive research on the representation of female characters in children's movies and TV programs ever done. Our results were astonishing, and bore out my observation that there was significant inequality: at that time, we found a 3:1 ratio of male to female characters in both family films and television shows aimed at kids. We've been data-driven advocates ever since, and have amassed the largest body of gender in media research focused on family entertainment.

> *We need to change what kids see on-screen. If it happens on-screen, it will happen in real life: life will imitate art.*

As a result of being awarded a technology grant from *google.org* a few years ago, we were able to pioneer and launch a machine-learning driven research tool to conduct and measure gender bias in film, television and advertising. In partnership with USC Viterbi School of Engineering, we developed GD-IQ (the Geena Davis Inclusion Quotient), which uses face and audio recognition software to analyse moving images and reveal data that is not possible to discern with the human-eye. For example, *GD-IQ* enables us to accurately measure screen and speaking time for gender, and race from face.

In advocating for change, the data does most of the work for us, because the people making media for kids love kids, and want to do right by them. By tracking and measuring female portrayals in children's entertainment media, we are able to influence industry-wide change. And we have been successful.

I was very surprised and disturbed to see the degree to which female characters are sexualised – even in G-rated films! Our study called *'Gender Bias Without Borders,'* the first ever global study of film, showed that female characters from 13 to 39 are equally sexualised. What are we saying to our youth about the value of girls and women when female characters are so often shown in sexy attire and/or partially or fully naked?

We recently achieved two of our top goals in this work: we've reached gender parity for lead female characters in children's television for the first time in history, and we've achieved gender parity for female lead characters in children's films for the first time as well. This reinforces to us that our theory of how to drive systemic culture change in this area works.

We still have a long way to go to achieve intersectional gender equity across the whole population of the fictitious worlds being created, but we are seeing progress – especially concerning race.

Geena's object
I like to keep little mementos from my projects. This nesting doll from the show *Commander in Chief* is my absolute favourite thing I've ever taken from a set. It's been almost 15 years and the character has really stayed with me. People still ask me if the show will ever come back, and I wish it would. Mainly because I'd get to reignite my fantasy of being the leader of the free world and I know how impactful it could be to have a character like that on TV today.

INVEST IN
PEOPLE,
NURTURE THEM
AND MAKE THEM
FEEL
PART OF A
TEAM
AND YOU
WILL ALL GROW
TOGETHER.

JUDY MURRAY

RELATIONSHIPS

Balancing what you need and what you get from all the people in your life

We know from our own research into women's fulfilment that broadly speaking, they value their relationships – with partners, friends, family, colleagues – above everything in life. This may be innate or due to social conditioning; for centuries women have been taught to be nurturing and responsible for the emotional wellbeing of others. We know for sure that studies reveal how women tend to invest more in maintaining their relationships and are more likely than men to share emotions and feelings with those around them.

At the same time women still carry the unequal burden of household and care responsibilities across the world. According to World Economic Forum this contributes not only to the gender pay and opportunity gap, but it is also a likely source of distress, making depression twice as common in women, worldwide. While women may seem to care more, they are working more in terms of emotional and domestic labour.

The women telling their stories on these pages reflect the extent to which we multitask home and work, but each in their way have endeavoured to change the limiting parameters of the domestic tradition, so that they can be freer to follow their purpose. We can learn from them.
Most of all, they show that relationships and connections are essential for success and fulfilment in all areas of life and that women truly rise when they champion and support each other.

The success of every woman should be the inspiration to another. We should raise each other up. Make sure you're very courageous: be strong, be extremely kind, and above all be humble.
SERENA WILLIAMS

JULIET STEVENSON

*I can express
who I am by being
other people.*

JULIET STEVENSON

Juliet Stevenson, who trained at RADA, has been nominated for many Olivier and BAFTA awards. She is known for her roles in films such as *Truly, Madly, Deeply* (1991), for which she was BAFTA-nominated and won the *Evening Standard Film Awards Best Actress* award. Her other film appearances include *Emma* (1996), *Bend It Like Beckham* (2002), *Mona Lisa Smile* (2003), *Being Julia* (2004), *Infamous* (2006), *Love is Thicker than Water* (2016) and *Let Me Go* (2017). She has starred in numerous Royal Shakespeare Company and National Theatre productions, including *Olivier* Award-nominated roles in *Measure for Measure*, *Les Liaisons Dangereuses* and *Yerma*. For her role as *Paulina* in *Death and the Maiden* she won the 1992 *Olivier Award* for *Best Actress*. Recent productions include *Happy Days* and *Wings at the* Young Vic, and *Hamlet*, *Mary Stuart* and *The Doctor* at the Almeida and West End. For the latter, she won the 2020 *Best Actress Critics Circle Award*. She also frequently appears on television. She received the lifetime achievement prize at *Women in Film And TV* awards in 2018. She was appointed CBE in 1999 for services to drama.

I grew up all over the world because my dad was in the army, so I never know what to say when people ask *'Where are you from?'* because I'm not from anywhere. I was born in Essex but when I was a few weeks old we went to Germany, then to Australia, then Malta, and then Germany again. So it was an itinerant childhood and I didn't really belong anywhere until I came to London at the age of 17. I guess I'm a Londoner now. I spent a lot of my childhood looking at groups of kids, thinking, *'I'd really like to join in.'* And then you do join in, and you make your mates, and then you leave, and move on, and start all over again. The only constant is the family, so I think that makes a very particular kind of family – a strong, binding force.

It meant I had quite a lot of time on my own, filling in the gaps when I didn't have friends. I quite liked that. I certainly have quite a big appetite now for time on my own – not that I get a lot of that, as the family is large and life is full, but I do have a happy relationship with being solitary. I loved my brothers very, very much. Sadly, I've lost my oldest brother. Now I feel my middle brother goes right back to my earliest days – he knows all the secrets. That's probably true of all siblings, but it's a very particularly shaped relationship; a relationship shaped around that shared,

shifting, itinerant childhood where sometimes we were all the others had.

I've often wondered whether there's a connection between that shifting background and the way I live in this job. You're constantly arriving somewhere new. Drama involves getting through the layers quite quickly, and I love that. I love making friends quickly, cutting through the small talk and the boring stuff, and having big conversations quite soon. I always feel very sad to move on. I like to make those bonds very tight, very close, very committed, for as long as they last. I regret them when I move on, and I'm happy to make them all over again. I love the fact that you're constantly meeting a new wave of people. It means you can make friendships across generations, across race, gender, sexuality – every kind of identity divide, you cross it. I think that teaches you so much, and perhaps helps to keep a sense of perspective on your own life.

Through other people's stories I can be who I am; I express who I am by being other people. I can't always do that as myself. I came from a very particular class; from a very limited, restricted upbringing; and I was a little girl who was very constrained by gender expectations and roles. I think I was busting to say and be more than any of those things were allowing me. I love trying to transform into other people. I don't like playing versions of myself all the time – it's boring, and therefore boring for audiences. I love transformation and I admire it hugely in many actors. I think it is what we're for. It's an interesting paradox: inhabiting somebody else's story, somebody else's circumstances and fears and hates and loves, and all the things that shape them, is a way in which you find out how you feel about the world – and you can lend your experience and recycle it into telling their story. We're like recycling machines: instead of paper and glass, it's life experience. The raw material of your work is yourself. Most jobs don't require your internal life to be the substance of your job. You can't please everybody all the time and that's okay. It's a job managing yourself – my wonderful partner Hugh has to pick me up sometimes, off the ground.

Practically speaking, being a working actress and a mother is really complicated. Looking back now, if I have a regret, I think I worked too much. When my first child was born, three months later I whipped her into the car and we were off doing a huge series filming. I took a wonderful nanny with me but I now look back and think, *'God, did I miss all sorts of things?'* I'm a very hands-on mother. I always wanted to have kids and I have adored all of it, including the challenges. That's probably the most important part of my life.

You can't please everybody all the time and that's okay.

But it is challenging, because work is an obsessive thing. Acting does absorb all of you. To make good work happen you have to completely immerse in it. And that's where it can conflict with parenting, because parenting is also pretty obsessive and immersive. Your children fill you up. The saying is: you can only be as happy as your least happy child. If one of the children is not happy, then I can't focus. I can't really be happy. Looking back, I think being a parent actually really helps the work.

I think psychologically it's made me much more stable; if I hadn't had children, I would have been much more vulnerable to the profession eating me away, eating me up. The frailties, the nervousness, the sense of insecurity, they constantly feed on you – I have often rooted myself back at home with the kids, and then none of it matters very much. What they are doing, who they are turning out to be, what they need day by day, are the really important things. The bruising of the profession, and even the triumphs, are pushed into perspective by them. Children keep you rooted and earthed.

Juliet's object
Aged about nine, my daughter went to pottery classes and she created this extraordinary creature with a strange, mythical horse's head. It's on ballet points and it's got one arm extended. It's such hybrid of animal, woman, human being, mythical creature, pet – a thing that embodied all her aspirations and all her senses of who she might be and what she might do in the world. I love it because it was made so freely, it was everything that she dreamed of in her scope of what a life might be. It had no boundaries, it was wonderfully ambitious, and wonderfully, uniquely hers. There's a degree of mystery in that object which I will never quite understand and that's somehow really appropriate to motherhood – we adore our children and we know them very well, but we don't own them and we never know all of them, and that's as it should be.

BOBBI BROWN

Bobbi Brown is a make-up artist, bestselling author, public speaker, entrepreneur, and the founder of Bobbi Brown Cosmetics – the initial 10 lipsticks that she created evolved into a global beauty empire. Since leaving her namesake brand in October 2016, she has launched four new businesses. In 2018, Bobbi launched her beauty and lifestyle website, justbobbi.com; she opened The George, a boutique hotel in Montclair, New Jersey, which she redesigned with her husband Steven Plofker and she created and launched Evolution_18, a line of beauty-inspired wellness products. Then in October 2020, Bobbi made her triumphant return to the cosmetics industry and launched clean beauty brand, JONES ROAD. Bobbi's many awards include the *Glamour Woman of the Year Award*, *The Fashion Group International Night of Stars Beauty Award*, and *The Jackie Robinson Foundation's ROBIE Humanitarian Award*. She was appointed by President Obama to the Advisory Committee for Trade Policy and Negotiation.

I grew up in the suburbs of Chicago, Illinois. I'm the oldest of three kids, and my parents were 20 and 21 when I was born. My dad was a lawyer, my mom a homemaker; we were a typical suburban family. I realised my parents were growing up as we were growing up. They got divorced after 20 years, but my childhood was pretty idyllic. Growing up, my mother was always around and there for me. I was really close to my family, my grandparents and aunt. I was social as a kid, and very involved in my group of friends.

I was bored at school unless there was a great teacher. I didn't excel in things that I probably should have. But it's all worked out. I told my mother I wanted to drop out of college. She basically said I couldn't, thank God. She said: *'OK, pretend it's your birthday. What would you want?'* which is the same thing as asking: *'What's your passion?'* I said I wanted to go to the department store and play with make-up. And she said: *'Why don't you go to college and study that?'* I didn't want to go to beauty school, but she said she was sure there was a college somewhere. Emerson College let you create your own interdisciplinary major. I know now that's called being an entrepreneur! You make stuff up, figure it out, and try things. It was the best experience for me, giving me basically a piece of paper that said I had to do certain things,

but the rest, I could figure out. That pretty much set me up for how I look at life now.

My mother was a knock-out – she was glamorous. It took me a long time to realise that, no matter what I did, I wasn't going to look just like her. Then, when I went into the fashion industry and was doing photo shoots with supermodels, I realised that at 5 feet tall, I wasn't going to be able to look like them either! I simply had to be me. That was a big, wonderful moment for me because it's when I became comfortable being myself. I realised that it's not about how you look. It's about how you feel you look, and that's such an important message.

> It's not about how you look, it's about how you feel you look.

Back when I launched Bobbi Brown Cosmetics, make-up was heavy, artificial, brightly coloured and very garish. My message couldn't have been more different. My mantra was *'looking like yourself was what's most beautiful.'* We made lipsticks that were the shade of your lips or, if you liked a red, pink or orange, they were muted, so they were flattering. Another big difference was that the line was created by a working make-up artist, not a marketing team – that was completely new and very ahead of its time and it was an instant success. We hit the ground running.

While I was launching my cosmetics line, I was also starting my family. By the time we sold the company, I had two kids, and then we had our third. I guess I was naïve because, when I became a Mom, I never really thought it was going to get in the way of my career. It forced me to quickly figure out how to multi-task. I was the person walking through the supermarket, carrying my baby, buying dinner, and on the phone talking to an editor. Somehow it worked out.

My husband taught me to never worry at night, because things look worse then: whatever it is, in the morning you'll figure it out. We share the mental load at home. Things don't stress him out the way they stress me out. I always worried most about the silly things at home but, after three kids, I learned you kind of figure it out. And I'm still figuring it out.

I always encourage people I work with to tell me what's happening at home, because of course I'm not going to call first thing in the morning if your child is sick. Communication is really important. For women who are working and starting out as mothers, so many things have gotten better and changed — you don't have to pretend that you're not going through it. Be thoughtful, be organised, and figure out how you're going to get it all done. I know it can be overwhelming at times but go slow and be patient.

I've been married 32 years, and I always joke that you should find out what pisses your partner off and not do it! I still aggravate my husband sometimes; sometimes he aggravates me. But I think when you've been together a long time you learn certain things. He taught me to say sorry: *'I'm sorry I upset you and I hear what you're saying.'* Just saying those words defuse the emotions and you can move forward. Sometimes I say *'truce'*

— because I'm not always sorry! — *'I wasn't wrong, but I'm sorry I upset you.'*

I get invigorated by trying new things. Most women I know are thoughtful, careful, and could probably take a few more risks. When you're in the thick of it, when you're working, when there are kids, when there's so much going on and you're balancing so many things, you are naturally more risk-averse. Men don't have to balance the same things that women do. Even if you're a high-powered woman, you have a lot to balance. Men don't have to worry about that. Being thoughtful and smart is what's going to make the biggest difference.

My advice to a woman who is thinking about starting her own business is to stop thinking and start doing. Even if it's not something that you're going to be able to complete right away, just start. Set your alarm an hour earlier. Do it on a weekend. That's how you become successful: once you start, you just keep doing it.

Bobbi's object
I have this necklace, normally with six different charms on it. Right now I'm wearing three Ds, because my kids are Dylan, Dakota and Duke. I also have an S for my husband Steven; I have a peace sign; I have a pawprint for my dogs; and I also have a charm with the date of 10.20, which was the day my non-compete (legal clause that meant she couldn't start another business) was up. I knew I was going to get back in the beauty industry once that date came. I keep all those close to my heart, and they show me where I'm going. The necklace symbolises how grateful I am that all of these elements are part of who I am.

191

JUDY MURRAY

*I put everything
into building great
team spirit.
To have confidence
in yourself you need
others who have
confidence in you.*

JUDY MURRAY

Judy Murray is a former Scottish #1 tennis player with 64 National titles. In 1995 she became the first woman to pass the *LTA's Performance Coach Award* and became Scotland's National Coach for the next 10 years. She created a National Development School programme, which produced 4 Davis Cup and 1 Federation Cup player, including her Grand Slam winning sons, Jamie and Andy. From 2011 to 2016 she was captain of Great Britain women's tennis team in both the Federation Cup and the Olympics. She has established many grassroot initiatives aimed at making tennis more inclusive and has shared her experiences as a player, coach and mother in a memoir, *Knowing the Score: My Family and Our Tennis Journey*. In 2020, she interviewed 10 of Britain's most successful sportswomen for the Sky Sports docuseries *Driving Force* to highlight the issues and challenges that still exist for women in sport.

I grew up in Dunblane, a village in Scotland. My mum and dad played county badminton and tennis and wanted me and my two younger brothers to enjoy sport. I was clever and, when I was 11, my parents sent me to a private school because there were better sporting opportunities. I played in pretty much every team – swimming, netball, hockey, badminton and athletics.

I always tell people it's not about what you have, it's what you do with what you have.

My mum was a tennis fan and we'd watch Billie Jean King on our black and white television, dominating women's tennis. Now, when I do events with her, I have to pinch myself! Fifty years ago, she changed the face of women's tennis when she made a stand with eight other women to break away and create a women's tour. She is the reason that tennis is the strongest women's sport in terms of equality of opportunity, prize money, sponsorship and visibility.

I had been set on becoming a PE teacher, but my form teacher advised against it: I went to university and did languages. Further down the line, when I was 27 and had just had Andy, we moved back to Dunblane and I volunteered at the tennis club where I had been a member when I was a kid. I taught teenagers to play and it snowballed. I ended up doing what I thought I would – teaching sport to children.

My kids enjoyed tennis and I wanted to help them improve. When Andy and Jamie were 8 and 9, I realised that they were exceptionally skilful but never thought that they would be world champions. In Scotland at that time, there was pretty much no infrastructure in terms of club teams and competitions, so I started to create some.

I went from working in the club to working in the wider district and I was the first woman to pass the *Lawn Tennis Association's* performance coach award. The Scottish National Tennis coach job came up, I applied and got it. The *LTA* course had given me information but it didn't make me a great coach. There were no top coaches in Scotland because there were no top players, and part of the reason was that there were no indoor courts. Nobody could aspire to be a great tennis player or coach because you couldn't play all year round. I was in the position of being able to create a structure and a coaching workforce and that is what I set out to do.

I knew that I had to start small and grow. I had a tiny budget and no staff; it was literally just me, a basket of balls and a block booking at a court. Parents helped when I couldn't afford to pay other coaches, we did trips down south and eventually brought in experts from other countries. Out of my little cottage industry, we got four *Davis Cup* players and one Fed Cup player, and Jamie and Andy did great things. A coach who started with me as a young girl went on to head up GB disability tennis, and another became head of men's tennis at the *LTA* and *Davis Cup* captain. I always tell people it's not about what you have, it's what you do with what you have. Invest in people, nurture them and make them feel part of a team and you will all grow together.

As a tennis parent, it's easy to get over-invested in your child because you are putting in so much time, so much money, so much effort to help them to improve. Because I was the national coach, I didn't get so caught up with my own kids. We nearly always travelled in packs and that was fun for the kids and much less stressful for me. Wimbledon in 2005 was a rude awakening. It was Andy's breakthrough year and suddenly the media got very excited and, sitting in the player box, we found ourselves being picked out on television. In opinion pieces about me there was sexism. I felt that if I was a dad of two competitive sons who were starting to find their way in the spotlight, I would be lauded and applauded – instead, I was a pushy, overbearing mum.

I realised that I needed to understand the media. So I did a three-day bespoke PR course; it wasn't just for me, it was so that I could help Andy to handle it. For me, it's always about the next step and what I have to learn. Over the years, I learned how to do massage and how to do tax returns in four different countries. I learned these things because we couldn't afford to pay anybody to do it. I went from teaching Andy and Jamie how to play the game, to how to handle the life and business of a professional athlete.

As a teenager I wasn't confident but that's changed – the boys' success was a big part of it and becoming *Fed Cup* captain in 2011 was huge. I had stopped coaching to concentrate on the boys' careers to give them the best possible chance to succeed. I became known as Andy and Jamie's mum and people forgot that I was a coach. So, when I was made captain, I felt recognised as a good coach. I put everything into building great team spirit. To have confidence in yourself you need others who have confidence in you. I build women up all the time, it is so important.

I have a completely different relationship with the media now. When my memoir was published in 2017, I did an extensive book tour and got a lot of confidence and release from sharing my story. Having had so many years of being bashed by the media, it helped to be able to tell people the back story and let them see the real me. I work hard and give back to my sport and always will, because I love doing it.

Judy's object
Sixty years ago, my dad went to Norway on a skiing trip. He brought back a gorgeous Norwegian cardigan with silver buttons for my granny. It's unbelievably warm and cosy and she gave it to me. If I am feeling a bit down, I take it out of the cupboard and put it on and it reminds me of what she would say to me if I was down: *'Get your chin out of your drawers and get on with it!'* I love that good granny advice: wallow for a short while, then find a way to change your mindset and solve your problem.

HANNAH FRY

Hannah Fry is an Associate Professor in the Mathematics of Cities. After gaining her PhD in Fluid Dynamics, she has published papers combining mathematics with criminology and architecture, as well as her 2015 book, *The Mathematics of Love*, which applies statistical and data-science models to dating, sex and marriage. The accompanying TED talk has been viewed millions of times. She is a best-selling author, writer for The New Yorker, winner of the prestigious *Zeeman Medal* recognising her work in engaging the UK public with mathematics, and an award-winning science presenter. She is also the host of numerous podcasts and television shows, with her expertise regularly called upon to develop and host BBC documentaries.

I think my ambitions were quite modest when I was growing up. It was much more about finding something that I really enjoyed and could try my hardest at. It sounds cheesy, but that was always really instilled in us; just doing your absolute best at all times. My mum said I should try and do my A-levels and see how it goes. So I did maths, physics and chemistry.

After I did my A-levels, I knew I wasn't quite done with maths. Then I did my degree, and then my masters, and then my PhD and I still really loved it. I ended up going back to do a postdoc and landed in this field of using mathematical ideas to look at human behavior. And it just so happens to be an area of mathematics that is full of all these secrets that are really compelling.

I started doing talks in pubs about things like sexual contact networks or about how gossip spreads, that kind of thing. And it just really took off. The more I did, the more people asked me to do. I had an entire year where I decided that I was going to say yes to every opportunity. And that essentially was the snowball that landed me where I am now.

My teenage self was very quiet, very self-conscious and lacking in confidence. All of the things that I have gone on to love, like physics, engineering, racing cars, computer games and programming, they just weren't really in my sphere. If my teenage self had been shown that these were possibilities, she would have been a lot happier. Maths is an incredible playground for your mind about who we are, how we behave, and how the world works. It's unbelievable that you can pack so much information about the world into this language that we've created to describe it. I'll never get bored of it.

When it comes to representation in STEM I would really like everybody, no matter who they are or what gender they are, to walk into a room full of scientists and feel at home. To feel science and maths is a place where they're welcome.

Hannah's object

There is a very significant object in my life, and it is a magic orchid, which is the source of all of my powers. I'm criminally bad with plants, but somehow this orchid has survived for decades. This orchid was given to me by my husband on the day of an exam as a good luck present. It just so happens that this thing blooms whenever stuff is going really well, like my TED talk, which got millions of views. And it was blooming when I got a big promotion. It reminds me that it doesn't matter how rational and logical you are in your work life, you are still human and still subjected to all of the biases and nonsense like magical orchids as everybody else.

GABBY LOGAN

Thankfully so many men are now brought up in families where they see women doing great things, and they realise women have just as much right to achieve their ambitions as men.

GABBY LOGAN

Gabby Logan is one of the UK's leading broadcasters and has recently been recognised with an MBE. The honour is for services to sports broadcast and promoting women in sport. A former international gymnast, Gabby began her broadcasting career in radio in 1992 and joined Sky Sports in 1996 where she quickly established herself as one of their key presenters. In 2004 Gabby hosted *Sport Relief* for the BBC before joining the corporation in 2007. While at the BBC Gabby has presented the *Final Score*, *Inside Sport*, *Invictus Games*, *Match of the Day* & *The Six Nations*, to name a few. She is now also a regular presenter for Amazon Prime Video's *Sport Fixtures*. Gabby is a prolific writer and has more recently entered the ever growing podcast world, launching her chart topping series *The Midpoint*.

My dad was a professional footballer so wherever we lived, he played for the club in that town, apart from when he played for Spurs; we never lived in London. If we were in Leeds and he was playing for Leeds, everyone wanted to approach him and have a piece of him and chat about the previous week's game. I grew up thinking that everybody chatted to everybody and my dad knew everyone.

I was born in Leeds and then we moved to Coventry, then to Canada, and back to Leeds. I'm one of four children, and my mum and dad both have a lot of siblings. Having an extended family and connection with the older generation was very important. At home we were very normal: kids all over the place doing different sports and activities.

I was pretty average at school until I was 11 or 12. And then a penny dropped, and I decided I could be clever and work hard and maybe do something with this education. I went to state schools, absolutely unexceptional schools, but I had some exceptional teachers – and I think if you can grab onto a teacher who can make you believe in yourself at the right age, it's a really powerful thing.

When I was about 10, I wanted to win Wimbledon, but then we moved to Leeds where there were no tennis courts, so I had to put that aside and find a new sport because in our family everybody had a sport and you were no one unless you were doing a sport.

I'd done gymnastics but they used to call me the baby elephant at home because I was always crashing into things. My sister started doing rhythmic gymnastics, which is different to artistic gymnastics, and I went along and really enjoyed it. The coach was a national squad coach and I suddenly found myself going for trials for regional squads and national squads and winning medals. For about six or seven years, I was totally devoted to this sport, training up to 35 hours a week and competing for Great Britain. But sport wasn't seen as a profession for women. Unlike my brothers, who thought they could be professional footballers, I didn't think I could earn a living from sport.

> *I grew up thinking that everybody chatted to everybody and my dad knew everyone.*

While I was doing gymnastics, I went on the kids' TV show *Blue Peter* to promote a competition. It seemed amazing, this TV world. I wondered how you got into it. My family was a blue-collar family. My dad had done well but nobody had a profession; nobody had been to university. I wrote to the editor of *Blue Peter* and asked how I could become a TV presenter. He wrote back, a letter which I have to this day, saying: *'Why don't you go to university? Then come back and see me afterwards.'*

I realised I was going to have to get some experience. While I was doing my A levels,

I wrote off to newspapers and radio stations asking for a week's work experience here and there. And then I went to university – I did law at Durham – and I met a guy who ran the radio station in Newcastle and asked if I could have some work experience. I called him within a few days of arriving in Durham and by Christmas I was reading the news and getting paid for it. By the time I graduated, I had almost three years of being a radio broadcaster, so alongside my degree I was doing a kind of apprenticeship in broadcasting.

When I graduated, they hired me to do the breakfast show, which is the flagship show on any station. It was a decent salary for somebody of my age. I thought I'd give it a year and, if it didn't work out, I could go off to law school and become a barrister. That hasn't happened yet. At the age of 22 I had endless energy. I was getting up at four o'clock to do the breakfast show and then the radio station said to me: *'You really love sport. You're always gravitating to the end of the office where the sports reporters are. Why don't you do the interviews on Saturday at St James's Park?'* – which is where Newcastle United play. I thought: *'Brilliant, I'll learn how to do these interviews and it'll be a nice Saturday job and a way to see the football for free.'* And then about a year later, Sky were doing a live game and they saw me and asked me to do a screen test for them to see if I could become a sports broadcaster – which had never been on the agenda because I didn't see how that could be a job.

Sky Sports was male-dominated when I first got there but so were plenty of places at that time. Once I started broadcasting, I realised that there was a reluctance among some people to accept a woman talking about sport. People would write columns in national newspapers saying how affronted they were by a woman talking about football.

When I moved to ITV, they put me in front of loads of big, high-profile football programmes.

I became the first woman to present a live television football match for them, and the first to front the Champions League. For the audience, it was new territory.

The highlight of my career was probably working on the 2012 Olympic Games. Coming from gymnastics, I've always loved the Olympics, and London was very special because it was our country coming together and putting on, for me, the greatest show on earth, celebrating who we were as a nation without being jingoistic or negative. It feels a long way from now because of everything that's happened since – but if you'd told 10-year-old me that that was going to be my job, it would have blown my mind. I don't look back and wish I'd enjoyed it more. I enjoyed every single second.

We now have an increasingly successful professional women's football league – and that's important, not because every woman wants to be a professional footballer, but because it's a reflection of our attitudes and how we show young girls that they aren't restricted in what they can do. Men have to come along on that journey. Thankfully so many men are now brought up in families where they see women doing great things and they realise women have just as much right to achieve their ambitions as men. I think we just need to keep collaborating. I really want to empower women; I also think we need to keep men in the conversation.

Gabby's object
I'm not very materialistic. I'm very lucky: I've got a nice house and enough clothes. I don't want stuff. I think the most important thing in my life is my family, and that all comes from the relationship I have with my husband. My engagement ring is the symbol of the ways we do things together. We're a team. Maybe because I'm from a sporting background, I know I wouldn't be able to do what I do without the team.

VANESSA KINGORI

*The biggest change
I would like to see
for women is a
repackaging of what
equality looks like.*

VANESSA KINGORI

Vanessa Kingori took up the post of Publishing Director of British Vogue in 2018, becoming its first female publisher in the brand's 105 year history and the first person of colour in the role in the history of the Condé Nast publishing house. She was previously Publisher of British GQ. Regularly cited by Powerlist as one of the *UK's Most Influential Black Britons*, she was appointed MBE for services to the media industry in 2016.

I was born in Kenya; I spent my formative years on the island of Saint Kitts, and from the age of seven I lived in London. My family is quite matriarchal, with lots of strong women. I grew up around an amazing grandmother, who was a blend of very soft and strong; a really loving, resourceful mum; and an incredibly smart, over-achieving sister.

Growing up, I found it hard to establish what my ambitions were. I absolutely knew that I wanted to be a mother, because I had these strong maternal figures around me. And my mother's a midwife, so there were babies around all the time. In terms of relationships, I was never the girl who dreamed of the big white dress. In terms of career, I didn't know – but I knew that I would carve my own path.

We need to stop hiding the female experience in order to level the playing field.

I had my son a year after starting the biggest job of my life: leading the business side of Vogue. Lots of people said, *'How will you manage?'* or *'Are you worried about keeping your job?'* A former colleague actually said, *'This is terrible timing, you poor thing. You won't be able to have maternity leave – you'll have to be back within a couple of months otherwise the wheels will come off; you won't be taken seriously,'* and people will say, *'This is why a woman has never had the role of running the Vogue business in over a hundred years.' You don't want to prove them right.'* It was really sad to me that another woman would put that

pressure on me. I just didn't take it on board. It's taken me a long time to know my worth and know that I add value in such a way that, if I'm going to be out for six months to a year, it'll be OK. I'll do the preparation and create the systems to make it work.

I made a decision early on to make sure that I nailed the job and was visibly a mother. I didn't have a template for how to do both so I reached out to lots of women I admired who'd had children at the height of their careers. And I was stunned that amongst the great advice some of these amazing, powerhouse women gave were things like: *'Don't have a picture of your child on your desk. Men can do that because it makes them seem more approachable. If women do that, people will assume every time you're not at your desk you're running off to your child.'* Another woman said: *'Don't ever refer to childcare or childcare issues.'*

All of these women were saying these things from a good place, based on their experiences and the challenges they'd lived. But I thought, *'There's a whole generation of women who have downplayed the fact that they're mothers in order to excel, so this is why there's no template. I'm going to make my life a lot easier, and, perhaps women coming through who want to have both a career and a family at the same time, I'm going to try to make it a little easier for them, by showing I am a mother, that I am doing all the things that mothers do, but I'm also doing a good job.'* I think that's really important and I would love to see even more of it from other women, it all helps us cheer each other along.

Achieving firsts is exciting and daunting, anyone who is talented and is breaking new ground has pangs of imposter syndrome. And that sometimes powers you to be better. But when you hear you're the first, a small part of you thinks, *'Am I trying to do something that maybe a woman can't do, or maybe a person of colour isn't suited to?'* I absolutely don't agree with that, but if you hear or feel it enough, it does seep in. I don't think about being first at this, or first at that: I think about delivering excellent results. My hope is that all under-represented groups will be more openly considered for leadership roles, if those of us who are first are seen. It can break misconceptions and hopefully inspire.

The biggest change I would like to see for women is a repackaging of what equality looks like. The women's liberation movement bravely fought for us to be able to do the same things as men in their push for equality. They were pioneers but in practice my life experience, and that of women I know, has taught me that fair and equal don't mean *'the same'*. Take the maternity process for example – how much women go through if they lose a baby, or if they're going through a pregnancy at work. These are experiences that are unique to women, men can not experience them in exactly the same way, we are not the same and we need a unique employment approach to give women the support and space they might need to recover and thrive.

I'm working with the *Royal College of Obstetricians and Gynaecologists* around the maternal process – things like endometriosis, fibroids often come up. There is so little funding and research, and such little consideration for how these things impact a woman's life, work and wider health. Many women also feel talking openly about these issues puts us at a disadvantage at work. For women to have an equal footing with men, we need some different considerations, so need the space to bring our whole selves to our roles, whether in the home or at work.

A lot of the things that we've been taught to hide away and *'push through'* are just part of who we are. We need to stop hiding the female experience in order to level the playing field and get the best from women.

I've been at *Condé Nast* now for 12 years. The past three years have been the most meaningful because I came on board at the same time as Edward (Enninful, editor-in-chief of *British Vogue* from 2017) with the same aspiration to dispel myths and normalise the marginalised. We've been able to power a new zeitgeist, showcasing empowered women, irrespective of body shape, physical ability, sexual orientation, ethnicity. In the media, we have been led to believe that if you are over 35, if you're over size 8, if you have a darker skin tone – a myriad things of things – you are less appealing and less valuable. To be part of shifting that narrative has been the most incredible and rewarding part of my career.

Vanessa's object
I treasure my grandmother's scarf. She had to leave school at 14 to pick cotton on a plantation in the Caribbean, long after slavery was abolished it was still there, figuratively. She was a prolific reader. She didn't travel until she was in her sixties, but she was in many ways the best-travelled person I'd ever met, because through reading, and being inquisitive and kind, she learned so much about other cultures, about other ways of being and living. It made her even more empathetic. She would wear this scarf to church; she would wear it to cover her hair when she cooked huge meals for our extended family and taught me to cook; she would wear it when she was tending her garden. The scarf is a symbol of a triumphant spirit and overcoming setbacks – and what real elegance can look like.

ANGIE GREAVES

Angie Greaves, *National Drive Time* Presenter, *Smooth Radio* and Smooth Sunday Mornings, has one of the most soulful and distinctive female voices in UK radio today. Angie began her career as an administrator at BBC Television Centre and moved to London's Capital Radio where she was discovered, by DJ David 'Kid' Jensen, who encouraged her into presenting. In 1990, she was the first DJ at the launch of Spectrum Radio and in 1992 she joined Choice FM and presented the *Angie Greaves Breakfast Show*. She then joined the BBC and presented shows on BBC London, BBC Three Counties Radio and the *Drive Time* show on BBC 2002 in Manchester. Angie became the first woman to join the *Magic* presenter line-up and after 14 years at the station she was poached by Global Media to join Smooth Radio.

I grew up in north-west London. We were the first Caribbean family on the road where we lived.

I kind of lost my way when my parents broke up, so I had no idea what I wanted to do. But I can always remember my dad telling me, *'Whatever you are going to do, do it well. If you sweep the streets, sweep them in such a way that when people drive past they go: Wow! Angela sweeps streets good!'* So I think that's probably the fighting spirit in me – the spirit of always wanting to do my best.

When people ask what I do for a living, I say, *'I sit in an empty room talking to myself, in the hope that somebody's listening.'* But it's using the art of communication to connect to people. You don't know who they are, you don't know what they're doing or how old they are – but knowing that you're connecting with someone, it's a beautiful feeling.

My big break in the UK came when I saw that there was a station called *Spectrum* with multicultural shows. *Choice FM* was being launched and I got a call asking if I was interested. I started temping in the week and doing one show on a Friday night. Then I was asked to do the breakfast show, and I never came off that show.

When it comes to black women in broadcasting and in management, I would love to see more women who look like me.

At some point, I would love to run a radio station, because it would mean girls seeing that it can be done. And that's what's really important.

There's a book called *The Four Agreements*, and I live by those four agreements: be impeccable with your word, don't take anything personally, always do your best, and never make assumptions.

Angie's object

My father gave this teddy bear, Rufus, to me when I was about eight. When my father was diagnosed with dementia, the teddy bear kept our conversations going. If I walked into his house on my own, he'd say, *'I recognise you from somewhere.'* If I went back to the car and got that teddy bear: *'Angela! How are you? Oh my goodness, you've still got that teddy bear!'* It brought him to life and the memories would just come clicking back.

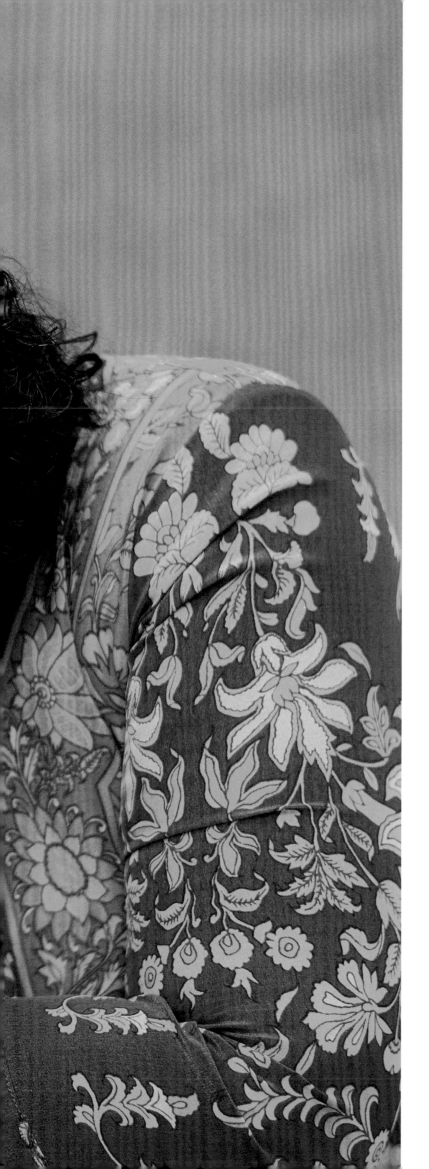

ASMA KHAN

I was going to change the world by cooking.

ASMA KHAN

Asma Khan opened her London restaurant Darjeeling Express in 2017, staffed entirely by Asian women, with a focus on working practices that are friendly both to women and to family life. The restaurant relocated to larger premises in 2020. She was the first British chef to feature in Netflix's award-winning *Chef's Table* series, in an episode that was Emmy-nominated, and is the author of *Asma's Indian Kitchen*. She is the founder of Second Daughters Fund, which encourages families in India to celebrate the births of second daughters.

I grew up in Calcutta. My family were extremely unconventional in some ways, because they allowed me to do whatever I wanted, but still raised their children to understand our culture, our religion and values. I have an older sister and a younger brother, so I am the second daughter. Being a second daughter is a very complicated thing. No one openly tells you it's not great to be a second daughter, but there's a sense of failure. Everybody's happy when the first child is born, whether it's a girl or a boy, but the old expectation is that the next one will be a boy, because a boy is a treasured heir. Unfortunately, in India, because of cultural reasons and the deeply patriarchal way that society is structured, girls are seen as a financial burden. No one celebrates having a second girl to look after.

Almost all the girls in my mother's family had an arranged marriage at 18, including my mother and my sister. When I turned 18, I told my mother, *'I'm not getting married, so let me go to college.'* I was allowed to study at Loreto College, an amazing all-girls college. It was an incredible experience. It opened my mind to a new world. Miraculously, my family found a boy who was willing to marry me. He was an academic from Cambridge. He was visiting Calcutta; we met and within three months we were married. I moved to England in 1991. I then studied law because I felt that it would make my parents very proud of me. I thought this was a way forward – to become a professional so that I would be taken seriously, and find a way to somehow find roots in this alien land where I'd ended up.

I cooked to feed people and I really enjoyed doing that. By the time I started my PhD, I'd had both my kids, and I knew that cooking was my real calling. I was going to change the world by cooking. I did supper clubs in my own house for three or four years; by that time I had a group of women who would join me in cooking. Then I took up an offer to cook in a very trendy Soho pub. In 2015, people didn't do pop-ups. I was a spectacular failure. I cried so much because I sold nothing the first day, nothing. But I came back the next day, and I thought: I'll keep cooking, somebody will enjoy my food. And that somebody was Fay Maschler, the Evening Standard food critic. She did a review and suddenly the place was packed. I realised that people want to eat my food, they're interested, they want to hear my story.

You are more than your dress size, your bank balance, your Instagram followers, the car you drive.

Then I met the man who turned out to be the future landlord of my Soho restaurant. I felt I had to get this restaurant, not for myself, but because there were no immigrant women talking about food on television or in the media, no one told their stories. We were completely silent. And I thought, *'I'm going to make this about every woman who's been marginalised and felt she didn't belong.'*

I opened a restaurant run by housewives. Our average age was 50. We were cooking for strangers as if they were our family. We were strangers in an alien land. Food had healed us, and I think all of us were trying to heal others, give them a sense of homecoming. Our restaurant became a place where you put your burden down. You left feeling healed, and empowered to see that good guys can win too. There is no aggression in our kitchen. We celebrate being women, being powerful but compassionate and empathetic in an industry where we are often sidelined and marginalised and abused.

There is no aggression in our kitchen.

Within a year of opening, I got a random email. I googled the name and it was the executive producer of *Chef's Table*. He said *'Why did it take you so long to call?'* And I said, *'I thought you were a hoax!'* Being on *Chef's Table* was, like Fay Maschler's review, life-changing. The whole world saw an all-female kitchen run by housewives and home cooks, where we talked about politics, power and equality without fear. We were fully booked for six months afterwards.

But when I looked at moving to new premises, landlords said, *'We don't have anything appropriate for you.'* I wonder if it was because I was not appropriate for them. Not a single landlord showed me a property. I had finance, I had tables booked one year in advance, but they wouldn't take a chance because I didn't have a business partner or a business plan: I was asked for my suited man with the money. Then the pandemic knocked everything sideways. I realised this was my opportunity. I went to the grandest and biggest property in Covent Garden. I told three young men in suits: *'Your whole life, you've had prejudices. Rise above them. Look at me, listen to my voice, and know that you can open the door and you can make a difference to how women are seen in my culture: immigrant women, Muslim women, female founders.'* And they gave me the lease. It was just incredible.

The fear of losing, of being laughed at and ridiculed by others, holds so many of us back. When people told me, *'You are so overweight that no one will ever marry you,'* or said, *'You are not graceful, you're not the kind of girl that our family is proud of,'* it did hit me — I did feel bad. I would tell myself, *'Pick yourself up.'* You are more than your dress size, your bank balance, your Instagram followers, the car you drive. You are more than that. I would tell my teenage self: one day, the world will know your name.

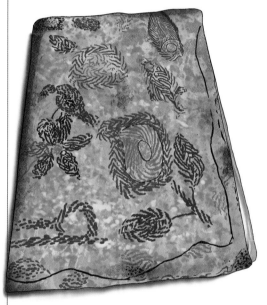

Asma's object
My diary full of addresses, from the time when there were no Facebook reminders. I didn't want to forget to send a card to my loved ones. It also contains poems and little prayers. It's covered in recycled sari material stitched together by women in villages in Bengal — the technique is called nakshi kantha. Something old and rejected is brought back to life by the stitching of beautiful patterns. I suppose I see myself in that! It's a diary of all the hope and aspirations I had. It's also the only place where some of the recipes in my family exist, because I scribbled down notes while watching my mother. Those scribbled notes are everything to me.

ASHLEIGH LINSDELL

*Support at home is
how you get through.*

ASHLEIGH LINSDELL

In March 2020, National Health Service nurse Ashleigh Linsdell started *For the Love of Scrubs*, a campaign seeking volunteers to make scrubs for frontline workers. Scrubs are the sanitary, easily laundered clothing worn by healthcare professionals. *For the Love of Scrubs* responded to a shortage of fabric scrubs caused by the Covid-19 pandemic, which saw doctors and nurses forced to wear uncomfortable, ill-fitting paper garments. She began the campaign alone, then appealed for help on social media. She was appointed OBE in October 2020 for services to the NHS; by then, more than 70,000 volunteers had made over a million personal protective equipment items.

I grew up in Honiton, a small Devonshire town. My ambition when I was at school was to be a dermatologist. I trained as a beautician, and then eventually as a nurse. It was a huge change from going through college as a beautician to moving to a nursing home, which is where I started my nursing career. I absolutely love my job – the patients I work with, the fact that I know how to be a nurse, and that I'm confident in really difficult situations. I developed a love for really acutely unwell patients and working in A&E. When I qualified, I moved into intensive therapy unit work, so I've spent the vast majority of my career working with really sick patients. There's something so humbling about working with patients who really depend on you, and on your skills and knowledge.

There's something so humbling about working with patients who really depend on you.

As with every job, there are areas where nursing is horrendous, from dropping a litre bottle of urine so your shoes squelch, to working six days in a row, so you're so tired you can barely walk. But there is so much that is empowering and wonderful that you come away happy, even in the worst situations. The best feeling you get is knowing that you've done absolutely everything you could for that patient. It doesn't always work, and I've cried with relatives, and I've held hands with people who are dying. I've done CPR for longer than

you'd even think was possible, so much so that your forearms burn and you can't bend your fingers, but even if you're not successful and the situation doesn't resolve in a way you'd like it to – and it doesn't always – knowing that I have done absolutely everything that I could is the best part of nursing and that's what makes me happiest at work.

My husband supports me in ways that I never thought were possible. He does a huge amount of childcare. In our family, it's definitely not the woman's job! He has cooked me roast dinners after I've finished nights, he has stayed up until the middle of the night to make sure my work uniform is washed, dried and ironed for the following day. When you're in the middle of your fourth night shift in a row and you're freezing and exhausted, knowing that you're not doing it alone and you have support at home is how you get through it.

The *For The Love Of Scrubs* campaign was a fluke. I still think, *'How have we done so much?'* In March 2020, I was working in a busy A&E department and Covid had just hit us. If you left the Covid area to use the toilet or go on a break, you had to change your scrubs and put a new pair on – and the scrubs weren't there. I came home and said to my husband, *'I have a sewing machine; I have material. I can make scrubs.'* I bought myself a pattern that made absolutely no sense and my first pair of scrub trousers were crotchless. I put out a call on social media to ask for help on sourcing wholesale material – nurses don't earn a huge amount of money so I didn't want to spend excessive amounts. Within a couple of hours, I had hundreds of Facebook messages saying, *'I'd love to help.'*

I would love it to be easier to be a mum in healthcare.

Someone suggested that I make a Facebook page, and within days there were 50,000 people wanting to help. We hit our first fundraiser target, £500, within minutes. We ended up with 143 sub-groups and 70,000 volunteers. Newspapers and radio stations got in touch, and Sky News turned up at my house with a camera crew. Chris Evans got involved, and he and his son Noah camped out in the garden and raised $1 million, and donated it in the form of fabric. It was surreal because I'm just a nurse, I'm not anyone special.

When I first qualified and I moved into intensive care, my matron on my first appraisal told me that I was bolshie. I had never been called bolshie before but it's probably the most accurate thing that anyone had ever said to me. Being told then, at the beginning of my career, that I needed to rein myself in a little was really important, because I learned that my personality could be quite abrasive and that's not how I wanted to be perceived. So that's definitely the best bit of advice I've ever received.

I would love it to be easier to be a mum in healthcare. I have been a nurse my entire adult life. I have missed out on so much of my daughter's life because of nursing. I can't just leave if they're short-staffed; I can't just say, *'It's the end of my shift, so I'm off.'* I missed the first time that she crawled, and the first time that she walked – things that don't mean anything to anyone else, but mean so much to me. Some days I don't see my child at all. I've left by the time she's woken up and I'm home after she's gone to bed. If I work

consecutive shifts, which has happened, there might be three or four days where I don't see her. It's really difficult.

After I had my daughter, I fell out of love with nursing. I was: *'Sod it, I'm going to go and do a law degree.'* I worked permanent nights with a one-year-old and did a post-graduate law degree at the same time. She had chicken pox during my exams. It was the worst year of my life. I hated everything about it and I gladly went back to the type of nursing that I love. I'd moved, I'd changed as a person, my perspectives had changed, so it was really good for me to have that break – but I won't ever be a lawyer.

The woman I admire most is my mum. She is the most amazing person; she is one of my best friends. We don't always get on – because you can't always – and she's very much like me, so we argue horrendously sometimes, but I know I could go to her with anything and she wouldn't judge me.

Ashleigh's object
The most important thing to me is my mum's eternity ring. Her fingers are now too large for it, so I have had it for several years and have worn it for quite a long time. I wore it when I graduated and when I got married. It's so unique and so personal. It represents the commitment that my mum and dad have. Marriage isn't rosy; it's not easy to be married to someone. But if I can have the marriage that my parents have, then I will be very rich.

THERE IS
NOTHING SHAMEFUL
ABOUT BEING AMBITIOUS
OR WANTING
TO EARN
A GOOD WAGE.

GINA MILLER

MONEY

Ownership, empowerment and open conversations about our finances.

There is no greater protection for a woman than money of her own. It is integral for our freedom and our equality, and yet women tend not to talk about money. Discussing money has long been seen as unfeminine or impolite, but the silence is detrimental. Worldwide a knowledge gap around finances keeps them dependent on men and this is fundamental to patriarchal structures that hold women in subordinate positions.

There is progress, although globally women still earn less and have smaller savings and pensions than men. The financial industry is adapting and high-profile women speaking out about their pay compared to male counterparts have brought the issue into the open. They have started conversations for other women; essential conversations that we need to achieve financial and gender equality. When we spoke to the women profiled within this book, we knew it was crucial to talk about the previously taboo subject of money. We have paid the price for our silence, so we need to keep talking.

We all know money is power. And women won't be equal with men until we are financially equal with men. Getting more money into the hands of women is good for women, but it's also good for their families, for the economy, and for society.
SALLIE KRAWCHECK

GINA MILLER

*Real freedom
requires you to be
in control of your
financial health.*

GINA MILLER

Gina Miller began her career in Marketing Consultancy, and co-founded investment firm, SCM Direct, in 2009. In 2012, she began the *True and Fair Campaign*, campaigning for reform and greater consumer protection in the UK investment and pension industries. She later rose to fame with her well-known legal case to defend Parliament's sovereignty arguing that the British Government could not start the formal process of the UK leaving the EU without seeking approval from Parliament. The Supreme Court ruled in her favour in 2017 and two years later, she challenged the Government for shutting out Parliament and won again, when the Supreme Court ruled that the Prime Minister's decision to suspend Parliament was unlawful. These cases are considered to be the most important constitutional cases for hundreds of years. She has been a social justice campaigner for over 30 years specifically in the areas of modern day slavery, domestic violence, special educational needs, online harm and the pathways that lead to poverty.

I grew up in British Guiana, which became independent Guyana a year after my birth. I was sent to the UK, to a small boarding school in Eastbourne, when I was 11. I was incredibly fortunate to grow up with amazing parents who taught me just about everything that made me who I am today.

After I'd been in the UK for a few years, Guyana imposed currency restrictions, which meant that my parents couldn't send any more money. They had a bit put aside, so they bought a small flat for my brother and me. My brother was 15 and I was 13, and we started living on our own. I wanted to help my parents, so I got a job as a chambermaid. It was joyous, not only because I was able to help my parents, but also because that independence of being able to buy things for myself at such a young age made me realise that money gives you freedom.

As far back as I can remember, all I wanted to do was to become a lawyer. My father taught me that law and justice are about how people live their lives and how you help people when they are in pain. I wanted to do that. So I went to university to study law, but about six weeks before my finals I was attacked, sexually, by a group of Asian men who thought I was being too Western. I was physically damaged and my entire life fell apart. I didn't tell many people because I was filled with shame. I felt somehow it was my fault and I didn't think anyone would believe me. I'm talking about 40 years ago.

I got lost for quite a number of years. I gave up on the law and on my dreams, and lived in a shell of myself. I had to go through a huge relearning of who I was before I could get back on track. I discovered that I was quite good at business, and coming up with ideas, and marketing, and being an entrepreneur, so that's what I went into. Regaining my sense of control was very attractive. And my early discovery that money gives you freedom drew me to financial services.

I worry about the world when we don't speak up.

I'm very passionate for women to discover that real freedom requires you to be in control of your financial health. As a country, we talk about a pay gap, but the pension gap is even more of a concern. Women have a bad relationship with money because that's the way society is constructed. Through the centuries, women have been told it is not their place to be in the workplace, to be in control of money. That's a social construct we still have a long way to go to dismantle. There is nothing shameful about being ambitious or wanting to earn a good wage, or wanting to be in a position where you can use your money to help others, to help society and to make a difference. Money is power and women should have access to that power.

When I had my first daughter, she was starved of oxygen at birth and I was told I should send her away to an institution. The lioness in me awoke. I fought my ex-husband, her father; I fought the institutions, I fought the doctors, I fought the authorities, and I kept her. Part of my battle was also ensuring that all parents could keep their children and get special support through the educational system. My first policy and campaigning battle was to get special education and what's called a statement for children who need it.

After years of being on my own, looking after my special-needs daughter and building a business, I was exhausted. Then into my life walked this man who promised to be a wonderful father and husband. What I didn't know was that, after our marriage, he would systematically try to break me. Again, I was at a point in my life where no one would believe me, because successful middle-class women don't suffer from things like that, and he was very much a pillar of society. After a few years of a very destructive, violent relationship, I had nowhere to go but I knew I had to leave. For three weeks my daughter and I lived in the car. That's when I decided that nobody was ever going to try and silence me or break me again.

Even though I didn't practise law, I never stepped away or lost my passion for the rule of law, justice, the constitution. I'm very interested in the abuse of power. My cases were not about Brexit, as people think, but about protecting our constitution. Those in positions of power tried to put themselves above the law, changing the way our whole representative democracy works. When I didn't

see anyone else stepping up, I decided that I was going to put my head above the parapet and do this. I really don't care what anyone thinks about me. In the days that I felt like giving up, the abuse that I suffered actually fuelled me to carry on. People ask me whether I'm fearless or brave. I don't think I'm either. I think I'm fearful, not fearless, that's why I speak up. I worry about the world when we don't speak up. I worry about the future for my children and for all children.

To any young woman, or anyone wanting to be a campaigner – you're going into battle. Take some time to really know yourself, your strengths and your weaknesses. If you know your weaknesses, somebody else can't criticise and tell you what they are. You just say, *'Yes, I know.'* It deflates their argument. Find how you are strongest. And no campaign can be achieved or won on your own.

My father was an extraordinary man and the best advice he ever gave me was that you're always going to be knocked down – but remember that you're the one who can pick yourself up.

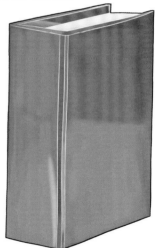

Gina's object
I'm not an objects person. It's been easier to walk away when life has gone wrong because I didn't have to take anything with me. When I was sent to boarding school, I had a little A4 album that I kept under my pillow. In it I had a photograph of my mum and dad, one of my siblings, and one of us all together. Every night I would kiss them before I went to bed. My little red album is my object. It is very precious to me.

GLORIA ALLRED

Gloria Allred is an American women's rights and victims' rights attorney and a partner in the law firm of Allred, Maroko & Goldberg, which has been the leading women's rights law firm in the USA for 46 years. She has represented many victims in cases of sexual harassment, rape, assault, child sexual abuse, and in cases of discrimination in employment. Ms. Allred's law firm has won hundreds of millions of dollars for victims in verdicts and confidential settlements. She co-hosted a radio show in Los Angeles on *KABC Radio* for 14 years, and her life and work is the subject of a Netflix documentary, *Seeing Allred*. She received the 1986 *President's Volunteer Action Award*; a *Lifetime Achievement Award* from *The National Trial Lawyers*, and was inducted into the *National Women's Hall of Fame* in 2019.

My father was a door-to-door salesperson. He never earned much money. My mother was a full-time homemaker, taking care of me. She always said: *'Don't grow up like me: have a career.'* My father never said what his aspiration was for me, but I'd say: *'I'd love to go to college, but I don't know if we'll have enough money for it;'* and he said: *'Don't worry about it. If you can get in, I'll make sure you can go.'*

I was very fortunate to be accepted into the Philadelphia High School for Girls. It was an all-academic, public, all-girls high school. We were told: *'You girls are the future leaders.'* I couldn't believe they were talking about me, with parents who only had an education up to eighth grade, but they didn't care where we grew up or what our circumstances were.

I met my husband-to-be in my first year at the University of Pennsylvania, married him the following year, and gave birth to my daughter the year after. I got divorced in my last year of college, but as a result, I have a wonderful daughter and two wonderful grandchildren. After my divorce, I moved back in with my parents. I became a schoolteacher, and while doing that job full-time, I commuted from Philadelphia to New York twice a week to study for a Master's degree at NYU. I was also teaching at the Cerebral Palsy Foundation two nights a week.

I moved to California and attended Loyola Law School in Los Angeles. There I met Nathan Goldberg and Michael Maroko and we decided to start a law firm. We are still together practicing law 46 years later.

We have won a number of precedent-setting cases, winning more than half a billion dollars for our clients, who are victims of injustice. We have filed lawsuits against many who have abused their power over women and minorities. At the end of 2019, a jury awarded our client $58 million for her sexual harassment by a billionaire, Alki David – one of the largest in the nation for one victim.

Women are still second-class citizens in the United States. We must fight for the passage of the Equal Rights Amendment (ERA), which states that *'equality of rights under the law shall not be denied or abridged by the United States or by any state on account of sex.'* We have been working to win the addition of the ERA to the United States Constitution since 1923. I always say that no one ever gave women any rights. We've always had to fight to win them.

Gloria's object
My object is a figurine of Ruth Bader Ginsburg, the now deceased United States Supreme Court Justice. She was and is a shero to me. I met her at the Supreme Court and sat next to her at dinner. I was surprised by her candour and how direct she was, but I was not surprised by her strong feelings about women's rights which she shared with me.

Ruth Bader Ginsburg

LUIZA TRAJANO

Photography by Jessica Mangaba

You cannot have innovation if you do not sit at the table with different kinds of people.

LUIZA TRAJANO

Luiza Trajano is a billionaire businesswoman named by Forbes as *Brazil's Wealthiest woman*. She is chair of the retailer Magazine Luiza, originally founded by her aunt, where she worked in various departments before becoming the company's CEO in 1991. Under her leadership, Magazine Luiza became a chain of over 1,000 stores throughout Brazil with over 18 million clients and 45,000 employees. She is the chair of Women of Brazil, a civil society organisation founded in 2013 by 40 Brazilian women entrepreneurs and dedicated to promoting equal rights. In 2017, the murder of an employee inspired Trajano to create a domestic violence hotline for her staff, providing counselling, legal advice and practical assistance for escaping abusers. She was awarded *Person of the Year 2020* by the Brazilian American Chamber of Commerce.

I was born in Franca, a city in the state of São Paulo, in Brazil. I enjoyed going to school. If there was a school trip, I was the leader. I was not thinking about leadership, it was just an urge to *'do something'* that I have had my whole life.

One of my aunts worked as a saleswoman in Franca, in a big, traditional store. In the old days, small towns had stores that offered everything from building materials to gifts and even banking services. She was in charge of a gift department and became well-known in the town. Her dream was to open a store and provide jobs for her family and that's how our company was created. My aunt was able to buy a small store, but she only had money for the first instalment. Then her sisters started to help; my mother and my other two aunts. And then a chain of stores was born.

I always say that I was born privileged because I was born in a family with four entrepreneur women. They had a great influence in my life. Seeing a woman with a job, signing checks, writing paychecks; it was all natural to me. A woman in charge, back then, almost didn't exist. So, my first role models were the women in my family.

I finished high school and went to college in Franca, but I already had a full-time job working in my family business. I started taking responsibilities and it never stopped. I worked for a long time in sales and then as a manager, but it was not my career plan. Back then there was no career plan; my career evolved naturally. I became a sales director and that was it.

To this day, I am one of the few female retail company CEOs. I have searched for female role models and I found some other female CEOs. We started to talk to each other and we started to meet. Now we have the group Women of Brazil, which is focused on women's strength in education, culture and health. Women of Brazil has global goals, and one is the fight against violence. Violence is a problem in the whole world. It is everywhere, not only in Brazil.

Nobody was talking about violence against women. The less you talk, the more women remain in silence, the more deaths occur.

I knew that a woman was killed every two hours, but we always assume it only happens far away from us. That was until a 37-year-old employee, a manager from Campinas, was killed by her husband while their son slept in the next bedroom. The next day I created a hotline for women in my company. We created a committee with clear goals and our first was called *'bursting the bubble'*. Nobody was talking about violence against women. The less you talk, the more women remain in silence, the more deaths occur. The hotline is so effective because the husbands get scared when they realise the company is protecting their wives.

We receive reports from employees to the hotline and it's men who help us the most. We worked hard on this and asked them to help. When they see a woman coming to work with bruises, they call our hotline. I am impressed at how male employees have helped with the programme. We don't want Denise's death to be in vain.

We support 20 institutions that fight violence against women all over the country. When we embraced this cause, it broke the stigma that companies couldn't talk about it. In the pandemic violence got worse, but the number of reports has increased. So, I believe we will see the results over time.

Magalu has always been a company focused on diversity. We started to talk about quotas; I am all for quotas as a transitory process to end inequality. We had been trying hard to get black people into senior positions. We had the idea of a trainee programme for black people and it was a success; we had 20,000 candidates.

There was a lot of controversy on social media about the programme, for being *'reverse racism'*. We were attacked on Twitter for 72 hours, but it created a shift and when you shift a paradigm, or a belief, you pay a price.

Hiring women and black people is not a favour anymore. Companies that don't change will not survive, because the market demands it. There is no innovation without it. You cannot have innovation if you don't sit at the table with different kinds of people.

I was not thinking about leadership, it was just an urge to 'do something' that I have had my whole life.

To this day I have a good relationship with all employees that do the hard work. I believe it keeps me real. I don't just sit in a pretty office just looking at the results. I never thought I was going to get where I got. I never said: *'I will be a woman who is a role model for Brazil'*. That is not me. I just do things.

Luiza's object
My object is a decorative elephant. I have a collection of them on my office desk and they were given to me as gifts. Each of them has a specific meaning to me and I associate them all with friendship and gratitude. Giving gifts is a habit that I nurture. It is a way of showing care and importance to others.

227

ROLLA KARAM

Rolla Karam is a television, film, and digital content expert with experience in sales, acquisition, content distribution and programming. She is currently *Interim Chief Content Officer* at Orbit Showtime Network, the Dubai-based pay-TV operator offering content in Arabic, English and Filipino. In March 2021, OSN launched a new channel, OSN Woman, all the content for which is curated by women.

Photography by Mohamed Dakhly

I grew up in Lebanon during the civil war. We were displaced repeatedly, and we lived in a series of different towns. We were always moving, just trying to stay safe. We went to Syria for a year. Every six months or so, my brother and sisters and I would change schools. Then, finally, when I was 14, we immigrated to Canada. We had to get used to a new country, a new culture, and the weather. It was freezing cold. It was a challenge but a safe challenge, at least.

I went to high school in Canada, then studied biology at university. From the age of 14 onwards, I worked to help support my family and pay my college fees. I always understood the value of money. It's important to me to work and get paid. I'm not saying money is everything, but it means you can take care of your family. You can be independent. You can help.

I originally wanted to do something in science but then I got married and we moved back to Lebanon, where I couldn't find a job in biology. Almost by chance, I went for a job in the media. Immediately, I loved it. I loved everything, from seeing the first ideas on storyboards through to the final shaping and the distribution.

I worked incredibly hard, putting in 20-hour days, and I was promoted to be an executive in the marketing department. In 2006, sadly, there was another war in Lebanon. I had two sons by then. I was scared. There was an opportunity in Dubai — and I got the job. I was now on the other side of the business, acquiring and licensing content.

In March 2021, on International Women's Day, we launched *OSN Woman*. There was no channel in the region for women, so we brought content from abroad. Our plan is to go on to produce original content in Arabic for the channel. We hope *OSN Woman* will give women a voice and a source of empowerment, leadership and courage.

Sometimes, in this region, there is an assumption that if you're female, you can't do certain things. We have this belief system that we inherit from our families that limits women. Even when you bring in revenue, people don't always believe you could have done it by yourself.

I am really inspired by women in this region. Many women in the Middle East have had really tough lives. In Saudi, we are witnessing a huge change for women, not because the government had eased the rules but because women fought hard to achieve this. I would really like to see gender equality in this region.

Rolla's object

My object is an album containing more than 100 letters. I've had them since I was 17, back when I fell in love with this guy in Lebanon and he used to send me letters in Canada. They're written in Arabic, by candlelight, because there was no electricity. They're not really love letters; they're about survival. They describe what he went through in the war. He's married now and doesn't even know I still have them. But if I have a weak day, I go back and read some of those letters and they give me a push.

LIV COOKE

*You've got to get so good
that you can't be ignored.*

LIV COOKE

Liv Cooke is a Freestyle Football World Champion and currently holds five world records in her sport. She achieved the fifth on record just four years on from becoming the youngest ever World Champion at the Super Ball Open Football Freestyle Championships. Since, Liv has gone on to grow an audience of over 6.5 million fans worldwide, landed numerous presenting roles on television and received the *Rising Star* award at the Houses of Parliament for her work. More recently, Liv has taken on a new adventure of property development.

I grew up in a small town called Leyland in Lancashire. At school, I was just your normal kid. I lacked a bit of confidence. I never liked it when the teacher asked me a question in front of the class. I have two brothers, who are four and five years older than me. As you can imagine, I've always been surrounded by sport, by competition, by jokes, by being wound up. I have to thank them, though, because they were always kicking a ball to me, and that led to where I am today.

I want to have an impact and help people the way I was helped.

When I was super-young, I used to say that I wanted to be an entrepreneur. I don't even think I knew what the word meant, but I thought it sounded cool. Once I could kick a ball properly, I wanted to be a footballer. I got into the Blackburn Rovers Centre of Excellence on my first trial, and the coaches were amazing. That step up was a big thing for me. It was my first experience of elite sport and realising that to make it to the top, you need to make it your whole life.

I was on track to play professionally, but I had a recurring back injury. I didn't want to come back as a bench-warmer, so I was in the garden trying to keep the ball up, trying to keep my touch and learn some tricks, and that was the start of my journey as a freestyler. I discovered videos online, and I started talking to a freestyler called Laura Biondo – and she was amazing. I put my heart and soul into it,

training all day, every day, for a year or two, until Laura said I needed to do a competition. I was like, *'No, no, no, I can't.'* She said, *'Liv, you'll never feel good enough. You're entering.'* And that was it. I went into my first competition.

That inspired me to train even harder and in the next competition, I qualified for the World Championships in Melbourne, which was a big deal – I was still the new kid on the block. I had quit college at this point and drifted from friends – I'd gone all in on my dream, so I knew I deserved to be there. A few days before the competition, I suffered an injury to my foot. In the final, that little injury went from a stress fracture to a full fracture. I'd just ranked second in the world; I said, *'I am coming back for gold. I don't care if I've broken my foot, I don't care if I'm out for five months. I know I'm capable of becoming world champion.'* And that's what I did.

When I was trying to build my career as a freestyler, I was often hired for women's football matches, to perform at half time or pre-game. I remember an agency saying, *'We want to hire you because you're female and it's a women's match.'* And I thought, *'Why not hire me because I'm a good freestyler?'* This even happened when I was ranking among the top 10 in the world, it happened when I was Vice World Champion and none of the guys could have competed with me. I asked myself, am I not as good as the guys? I had a better ranking and I'd beaten them. Am I not as appealing? I've got more followers. Do I cost more? No. I just

232

couldn't wrap my head around it and it felt so unfair. In those situations, I think you've got to get so good that you can't be ignored, and that's exactly what I did.

I like to make money, unapologetically. I've been on shoots where they've talked down about a woman who's wearing lots of jewellery or drives a flashy car, but then a man's praised. Why is that a thing? I just wish for a world where a girl can drive a Lamborghini and not be asked if her dad bought it. Or where a woman can be a CEO and sign deals and tell people what to do without being called bossy. Or where we can just chase our dreams. It's what we deserve. I'm not asking to be given extra credit or be paid more than a man. I'm just asking for equality.

There's a lot that I still want to do. I want to get better physically, I want to get better mentally, I want to be a better friend, I want to be a better role model. I want to get better with my videos, my content. And I want to have an impact and help people the way I was helped. The feeling Laura Biondo gave me when she replied to my message – I want to give that to my fans. They've given me my career; they've given me everything that I am. So I want to make something for them. I also want to give back to the beautiful game, to grassroots football, so I've got a mission to make that more accessible for everyone. The cost of hiring a 3G (high-quality synthetic turf) football pitch in the north of England is £200 an hour. How is that fair? People talk about making the game more accessible, but the one facility that people need is extortionately priced.

I don't experience imposter syndrome when I set my own goal and go after it, because I have set the target. But I experience it a lot when it's something external, like an award

or recognition that I didn't plan for, even being asked to be a part of this book among incredible women. Sometimes it takes an external voice to counteract that – a friend who reminds you that what you achieved was actually pretty good.

My advice is to go after whatever you want.

My advice is to go after whatever you want. If you want to go into football, you want to go into freestyle, you want to go into ballet, television, business, economics, finance – whatever it is, just do it. Why not? Who says you can't be the best in the world?

Liv's object
The football is the object that has given me everything. When I first discovered football and joined a team, it gave me confidence, social skills and friends, and I grew as a person. The same object travelled with me as I overcame setbacks and found passion in freestyle, which has given me my career and taught me so much about life. I don't think the best part about winning the World Championships was the trophy, I think it was the person that I became.

CARLI LLOYD

Photography by Brad Smith, ISI photos

*It's about embracing
who you are as a
person. There should
be no comparisons
with anyone else.*

CARLI LLOYD

Carli Lloyd is an American soccer player, two-time FIFA Women's World Cup champion, two-time Olympic gold medalist, and two-time *FIFA Player of the Year*. She went to Rutgers University, graduating in 2005 with a degree in Exercise Science and Sports Studies. That same year she joined the United States Women's National Team. In 2016, she detailed her journey in a book, *When Nobody Was Watching: My Hard-Fought Journey to the Top of the Soccer World*, which went on to be a New York Times best selling memoir. She was also named Member and co-Chair of the President's Council on Fitness, Sports, and Nutrition by President Barack Obama in 2016.

I grew up in Delran, South Jersey, just outside of Philadelphia. It was a hard working, blue-collar type of town, a very small working-class neighbourhood. Everybody knew everyone. My dad worked in a machine shop. My mom was a paralegal secretary. And it helped shape who I am today.

I was a very hard worker. I wasn't gifted with smarts, but I worked hard to earn As and Bs and was a really good student. I was kind of funny in school, and I liked making people laugh. Gym was probably my favourite class because that's when I could really be myself and be active and competitive. I loved it. I was just a typical tomboy who loved playing every single sport.

I was always outside playing and I was super passionate about soccer. Everything was all about the ball. And that laid the foundation for me to have this career. I didn't have anyone in the family that played soccer besides my older cousin Jamie. It was just something that I loved doing. My biggest thing was being competitive, wanting to do things that I couldn't necessarily do at first. I just loved being challenged.

I started playing soccer at the age of five. My parents just got me involved in the local team in my town. I played for several years there, then moved to a travel team in Delran. It got to the point where we had to figure out what was going to help me to be seen at college level. My parents and I decided I should try out for the Medford Strikers Soccer Club,

and I was on that team from the age of 14 until I went to college.

I was seen by hundreds of colleges all around the country. I also played New Jersey ODP, which has the best players from Maine to Virginia. Once you make ODP, you then can try out for the regional team. It was when I made it to the United States Under-21 team that I was selected to try out for the full *Women's National Team*. And that's how my career evolved.

The minute I started with the national team, I decided I was going to work incredibly hard every single day. I made a vow to myself to never switch off. I was going to train harder than any other player, make sure I was taking care of my body, having ice baths and massages, getting plenty of sleep, and making sure I was eating well. My exercise routine usually consists of a long aerobic run, followed by a session with my strength guy, another session on my own, then skill work and sprinting circuits.That's all on top of my team training. I usually have one day off a week. It's a lot of consistent work. You never play a perfect game, so I get to try and be better every single day.

I've missed out on everything; holidays, vacations, birthdays, anniversaries, funerals. There's really no time to switch off. But I've also had this unbelievable career, and I've been able to compete in World Cups, compete in the Olympics, travel the world, meet so many different people, have so many doors open up. So it's all been worth it. It's something that I will cherish forever.

Never let an obstacle or failure hold you back. Embrace it, learn from it, work through it and compete against yourself.

I'll never forget the 2015 World Cup in Vancouver. We were playing in the US on home soil, and I scored three goals during that game. To win that game with my teammates was an unbelievable moment. It had been 16 years since we won the World Cup. It was indescribable. It was just amazing to hear the crowd cheering and showing their support.

The best part of being in a team is embracing each individual. Every player has a unique, amazing talent and brings something super special to the team. We're all fighting for one common goal, and that's to win games and win championships together. Everyone needs to bring the best version of themselves to the field, and then collectively, you all have to come together with that fight. I think that's really cool. I just love the camaraderie and pushing each other every day to become better. You get to be a part of something that's bigger than yourself.

For some people it's hard to afford to get involved in sports. We need to find different avenues and opportunities for all people, whether you have a lot of money or you don't. I think that's so important because those that don't have the opportunity to join a team are missing out. We need more opportunities and more support for everyone who's interested in soccer.

There are many women all across the world that inspire me. I extract things that other women have done throughout the years. But I don't try to be somebody I'm not. I just strive to be the best possible person and player that I can be. I think the most important thing,

regardless of whether you're playing football or not, is being your authentic self. We live in a world with social media and the pressure of having to look and act a certain way. We worry about who likes us, who doesn't like us. But it's just about embracing who you are as a person. There should be no comparisons with anyone else.

Never let an obstacle or failure hold you back. I look at obstacles and failures as an opportunity to propel you towards success. Embrace it, learn from it, work through it and compete against yourself. Work extremely hard. Try to be better every single day and follow your dreams and goals.

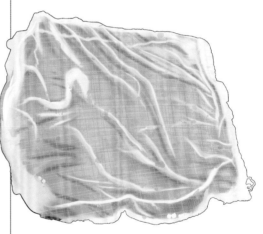

Carli's object
Growing up, the thing I always had with me as a baby and a young girl was this blanket that was given to me. I don't know why, but it just made me feel safe. I still have it; it's in a box and it's almost disintegrating. My parents said as soon as I got it, it went with me everywhere. That blanket triggers a lot of memories for me, a lot of good times as a child. I had it outside with me on the lawn, in the car, in my crib. And it's kind of weird because when I stopped having that blanket, it was a soccer ball that I brought with me everywhere. I don't know why but my safe place went from the blanket to the soccer ball, which I think is pretty unique.

237

VICTORIA DERBYSHIRE

*The secret to my success
is that I've always worked
really hard.*

VICTORIA DERBYSHIRE

Victoria Derbyshire is a journalist and broadcaster. Her award-winning eponymous BBC TV current affairs programme ran from 2015 to 2020, and she has also presented *Newsnight* and *Panorama* for the BBC. She appeared in ITV's *The Real Full Monty: Ladies Night*, an entertainment documentary to raise awareness of breast cancer. The programme won an *International Emmy*, a 2019 *Royal Television Society Award* and was BAFTA-nominated. Before the *Victoria Derbyshire* television programme launched, she was a BBC Radio 5 Live presenter for 16 years. She won *Sony gold* awards in 1999, 2002, 2010, 2011, 2012 and 2014, a *BAFTA* in 2017, and two *Royal Television Society* awards in 2018. The *BAFTA* and one of the RTS awards recognised the significance of a powerful interview with victims of abuse from football coaches, which led to perpetrators being jailed.

I grew up in Lancashire, in the north of England. My mum, my younger brother and sister and I were really close-knit, partly because my father was not a particularly brilliant father. He didn't treat us very well at all. But we had fun, we had a laugh; we loved each other; we looked out for each other.

I try to do the kind of journalism that can contribute to righting a wrong.

My mum was always really encouraging and wanted to give us as many opportunities as possible. She would take me to drama, dancing, swimming, and karate – absolutely everything that you could possibly wish to do when you were a kid. I remember her saying when I was about 13 or so, *'You could be a barrister or a lawyer because you're really good at arguing.'* So that was in my head for a bit, and it was only when I got to university that I really started to formulate ideas about journalism. I was writing for the university newspaper, but I didn't think I was that good a writer, so I started to investigate if there were other ways of being a journalist. I realised that you could go into radio or television, or both, and it went from there.

The secret to my success is that I've always worked really hard. I'm always asking questions, trying to better myself, trying to learn – I'm still learning. Also, I've asked people for opportunities, because I've always thought, *'Well, the worst that can happen is they say no.'* Quite often the jobs that I've got are because I've said, *'What about this as an idea? Couldn't we do this?'*

I am moved by people who haven't got a voice, so I've always been drawn to that, hoping to give people a voice. I try to do the kind of journalism that can contribute to righting a wrong. It doesn't always work but you can only do your best.

I decided to record my treatment through breast cancer because I'm a journalist. I approached it factually: this is what happens when you have a mastectomy; this is what happens when you have chemotherapy. Obviously, going through this treatment, there were lows. I thought: *'OK, I've got to be honest about this, how I am affected by this treatment and the side-effects'* – my hair falling out or feeling incredibly low because chemotherapy wipes you out. Or how I felt about losing a breast. As it happens, I was more distressed about losing my hair than losing a breast because I thought, *'I just want the cancer out of me.'* I felt it helped me continue to be a journalist and not only to be a cancer patient.

When I was doing my video diaries, I realised that cancer was often a taboo subject for a lot of people. People whisper when they say the word cancer. Part of the thinking for the video diaries was: if I can normalise this, then maybe it diminishes it. It takes away the power a little bit from the big C. It helped to take a day at a time. I didn't want to think too far ahead, about how long treatment might take – and I was one of the lucky ones, my cancer was treatable.

Women have to get over their reluctance to talk about their wages.

I would hope my teenage self would be really happy that I have ended up doing a job I absolutely love. Compared to some women, I think I've been pretty lucky as I've not really experienced much sexism, just small instances – apart from one time when I realised a male colleague doing exactly the same job as me was being paid way more than me. This was nearly 20 years ago. To my shame, I didn't realise this was illegal; to my credit, I went to my boss and said, *'This isn't fair, this isn't right. We're doing the same job, we're as good as each other, and I am being paid far less than him.'* If I'd known it was illegal I would have said so; as if was, over weeks and months – it was hard going – I persuaded my boss to increase my salary. It still didn't match my co-presenter's but I made some progress. And I got to a point where I thought, *'I've achieved something. I'm going to leave it now.'* Gosh, if I had my time again, I would have kept on going until we had equal pay. Anyone going through that now, do your research, do your due diligence, find out whether you're doing the same thing, whether you've got similar skills, and then ask for equal pay.

Women have to get over their reluctance to talk about their wages. It's really important. I hope we've made some progress towards being much more open about saying, *'OK,*

my wage is this, what's your wage? You're doing the same job as me. Can we check? Can we compare?' And once you've got that information, then you're absolutely within your rights and you have the protection of the law to respectfully say, *'I would like to be paid equally, please.'* Earning a wage means that you have independence, it means that you have options, it means you can provide for your family. It means the same for women as it means for men, so pay us equally. My absolute favourite piece of life advice, which I still follow, is: never, ever give up.

Victoria's object

I've chosen my diary. I have written a diary since the age of nine, and I've got 40-odd stacked up. I've always really liked recording what was going on in my day. It helped me make sense of it, not just the bad times but the good times as well. When I was young, it was about what I did at school and what I wore to a party and which boy I fancied. As I started to grow up, I recorded news events. Writing a diary has helped me make sense not only of my own life but also of what's going on around me and I've found that really helpful.

KAREN BLACKETT

*Modern Britain is a
beautiful fruit salad.
Unless you're creating
brand stories and corporate
stories that reflect your
consumers, you won't be
listened to.*

KAREN BLACKETT

Karen Blackett works in the advertising industry as CEO of GroupM UK, the world's leading media investment company and is also Country Manager of WPP UK, the world's leading marketing communications organisation. Karen began her career in media planning designing how media should be used for her clients' campaigns. Named by Vogue in 2018 as one of the *25 Most Influential and Inspirational Women*, in that year she also topped the *EMpower 100 Ethnic Minority Executive Leaders* list and was appointed the Race Equality Business Champion by the UK Prime Minister. She is a Non-Executive Director for the UK Government Cabinet Office, and sits on a number of boards including the Creative Industries Federation and Creative England. Karen was the first alumni to be made Chancellor of the University of Portsmouth in 2017. She was awarded an OBE in 2014 and was named in 2020 as one of the 100 *Great Black Britons*.

My mum and dad really believed in the power of education. They were first-generation immigrants from Barbados who came to the UK in 1961. My dad worked as a bus conductor before getting an apprenticeship with BT as an electrical engineer. My mum trained as a nurse and worked in the Royal Berkshire Hospital for 35 years. I grew up in Mini Barbados, which, for those who don't know it, is Reading.

Our house was always full of people from the Caribbean and the food, music, and stories of Barbados. My dad was one of the biggest feminists I've ever known, which is rare for a first-generation immigrant West Indian man. He knew my sister and I would face prejudice on account of our gender and our race, which is why my parents held on to a belief in education – because if you have professional qualifications, no one can take them away from you.

He encouraged us to celebrate our difference because, he said, we were always going to stand out. *'Get comfortable being memorable,'* he said, *'because you're going to walk into a room and be one of only a few women, and probably the only person of colour. No point in trying to blend.'*

As a child, I was fascinated by advertisements. I'd sit in front of the television trying to come up with better ideas. In the car with my dad, I'd try to improve the radio jingles. When I left university, I researched advertising, subscribed to the industry magazines, and applied for loads of roles, getting rejection after rejection. Then I saw an ad in the Independent for a media auditor. I wasn't sure what that was, but it had the word *'media'* in it.

One of my sister's friends was a junior brand manager and knew something about it, so I quizzed her and went for an interview. At that stage media auditors were inside media agencies – and I don't know what the interviewers saw, but they said, *'We think you might be better in a different part of the agency.'* Auditors assess whether advertising campaigns have hit their targets. I would have been a rubbish auditor, a frustrated creative.

If our industry is to survive, the people creating the stories and behind the cameras as well as in front of them must reflect society. Thirty-one per cent of all kids under the age of 10 are mixed race; it's the fastest-growing demographic. Modern Britain is a beautiful fruit salad. Unless you're creating brand stories and corporate stories that reflect your consumers, you won't be listened to. Diversity is not a problem that has to be fixed; it's the solution for growth.

I'm sick of hearing, *'Well, we simply can't find people.'* You need to look properly. In a number of industries, not only mine, there's a habit of going back to the same universities to recruit. Rather than waiting for people to come to us, we need to go out and look for them. It's not that hard if we partner with organisations that understand the communities we want to attract, like the Brixton Finishing School or Rare recruitment.

I talk a lot about work-life blend, because balance makes it sound as though there are winners and losers.

My advice to anyone starting out is to network. It sounds like a grubby word, perhaps something to do with going to pubs and restaurants, which is no use if you don't drink or don't have the time, capacity, or availability. But networking can be all sorts of things: going to a training programme, or an event, or talking to people on social media. If you have an opportunity, always try to say yes, because you never know who you might meet. Some of my cheerleaders, the people who help me through and encourage me when imposter syndrome hits, are people I've met that way.

In the past, the most senior, global roles in my industry have gone to men who could travel two weeks a month. The pandemic has shown us other possible ways of working. I was very clear, when I said I was pregnant, that I was ambitious as ever, that I intended to be even more productive, but that I was going to work in a different way. I was promoted 11 months after having a child, and I was a single mum. I had the support of a boss who saw what I was capable of. To this day, I don't think he realises I'm a woman and I'm black. He just saw talent.

I have a role I love in a creative industry. It doesn't feel like a job. Yet I'm fully aware that predecessors in my role were probably paid more than me. I advocate in my

organisation to eradicate any gender pay gap. Will it happen in my career lifespan? I don't know. Will I give it a bloody good effort? Yes, I will, because there should be a salary and compensation package for a role. Gender or race shouldn't come into it.

I talk a lot about work-life blend, because balance makes it sound as though there are winners and losers. It's something I have on my email signature: *'I'm sending this email at a time that works with my work-life blend but I don't expect a response outside of business hours.'* I don't enforce what works for me on other people. Too often, organisations have a template of how people should work, rather than thinking about how to get the best out of them.

I'm not Wonderwoman. I see asking for help as a sign of strength. I'm also aware that when male colleagues see women working and performing really well and embracing being a mum, that changes their minds about what working mums can achieve.

Karen's object

My significant object, which sits on my desk at home, is a little pair of silver-coloured baseball boots my son had when he was about nine months old. My passion for diversity, equity and inclusion was really let off the leash when I had him, because I don't want things to be as hard as they once were. I want to ensure he's judged by his character, not his colour. He has made me more fired up to change the world.

245

'FINANCIAL INDEPENDENCE IS KEY TO WOMEN'S FREEDOM'

Introduction from Ann Cairns, Executive Vice Chair of Mastercard and Global Chair of *The 30% Club*.

Financial independence is key to women's freedom. When we have the ability to earn a decent wage, to own and protect our property, we have choices.

I'm an engineer by background and was the first woman to work offshore in the UK oil and gas industry but I've spent the past 30 years working in financial services. My experience of the industry has been both hugely satisfying but at times very challenging. It was my job to see Lehman Brothers through the bankruptcy process that happened during the financial crisis of 2008, a time I witnessed the industry on its knees. On a more personal level, I've often been the only female executive at the table and have even had my abilities as a mother called into question for no other reason than I have chosen to work.

However, the highs have far outweighed the lows. A recent and significant high was my involvement in Mastercard's becoming the lead investor in the $100m Astia Fund, which provides early-stage venture capital for startups that include women. In the US, startups with all-female founding teams secured just 2.4% of venture capital funding last year.

There's so much the financial services industry has to offer women, in terms of both a source of employment and its contribution to society by designing products and services with women in mind. This has never been more important since the Covid-19 pandemic, which has stolen not only lives but livelihoods.

But in spite of this, women still control two-thirds of all household spending. In fact,

so great is our collective purchasing power that recent research suggests financial services companies are missing out to the tune of $700 billion a year by not fully meeting our needs as customers.

Women are more educated and have more opportunities than ever before yet female financial inequality remains significant all over the world. In the UK, women earn 15.5% less than men on average. Our pension pots are 30 to 40% less than men's and we're more likely to be in poverty in retirement.

The tiny number of women in charge of financial services companies is another aspect I think about often in my role as global chair of the *30% Club* - a campaign to boost female representation at the highest levels of business. In the UK only 6% of financial services CEOs are women, according to the Oliver Wyman Women in Financial Services 2020 report.

But things are changing for women in the industry for the better. The numbers of women on the boards of UK financial companies has grown to around 23% in recent years.

Organisations increasingly realise that diversity is a business imperative, often leading to better decision making and better financial performance. And financial institutions are increasingly committing to improving outcomes for women as both employees and customers.

The women featured over the next two pages are some of the most admirable and inspirational across the world of finance. They give me hope that millions of girls and women will be better off tomorrow and have more choices to make because of the action these women are taking today.

HSBC

HSBC is one of the largest banking and financial services organisations in the world. With customers, suppliers and communities spanning many cultures and continents, HSBC continuously looks beyond its own business, to measure against the high standards set by experts and industry benchmarks in order to continuously develop and improve. HSBC works hard to ensure that its workplace is a diverse and inclusive space that reflects the communities it serves, wanting everyone to achieve their full potential – regardless of their gender, ethnicity, disability, religion, sexual orientation or age – because, for HSBC, failing to build an inclusive organisation in which everyone has the opportunity to fulfil their potential is completely self-defeating.

Susan Yau is a Senior Audit Manager for HSBC and has managed and led audits focusing on Commercial Banking for Europe, Middle East and Asia. The audits are across multiple risk areas including Financial Crime, Credit, Fraud, Model, Conduct and Sustainability risks. *I want to make sure that people from all backgrounds have access to finance, understand their career choices and can work at it from a younger age.*

Zoë Knight is a Managing Director and Group Head of the HSBC Centre of Sustainable Finance. Zoë has advised global institutional investors on equity investing and climate change for over 20 years. *The essence of never stopping learning and being curious about what's going on around you is so important. But always be true to yourself. Hold on to what you believe in and be true to your purpose and values.*

Janet Henry was appointed as HSBC's Global Chief Economist in August 2015. She recently became a Governor of the UK's National Institute of Economic and Social Research and is a member of the World Economic Forum's Chief Economists Community. *I was so happy when a man on my team, after becoming a father, asked me if he could go down to four and a half days a week. Once men start taking on more flexible arrangements, there will be less stigma attached when women ask for those flexibilities. The more flexibility, the more women can be involved at senior levels.*

꩜ BARCLAYS

Barclays is a British universal bank that deploys finance responsibly to support people and businesses, acting with empathy and integrity, championing innovation and sustainability, for the common good and the long term. Barclays is committed to harnessing the power of diversity and inclusion in the business, trusting those that work there, and valuing everyone's contribution. The company understands that creating an inclusive and supportive culture is not only the right thing to do, but also what is best for the business, making Barclays better at understanding the needs of customers and clients, and creating a sense of belonging and value that enables employees to perform at their best.

Kirstie Mackey is a Managing Director who is Head of Citizenship & Consumer Affairs for Barclays. Kirstie is responsible for driving citizenship, which comprises UK retail banking, consumer credit cards, wealth and business banking. *The advice I would give to myself if I was a teenager is to be ambitious and be bold, but also don't be afraid to take risks because taking risks and making mistakes is ultimately who you become and that does shape your personality.*

Karla Maloof leads the International Corporate Banking coverage effort for Barclays' Insurance, Healthcare and Consumer Retail sector teams in the Americas. Karla serves as Co-Chair of Win, the gender network and is passionate about education and promoting diversity in the workforce. *Be curious, lead with integrity and really believe in yourself. It's important to build a network, create a circle of connection that can help you test out ideas and talk through challenges. You are in control of your destiny so be your own best advocate.*

Zainab Kwaw-Swanzy is a Senior Digital Product Manager at Barclays UK and Co-Chair of the Barclays Black Professionals Forum (BPF) which champions diversity, inclusion and equality in the workplace. *Imposter syndrome is real especially if you're a black woman in spaces that aren't diverse, so I sometimes question if I'm doing things right and if I'm doing things well enough, but I try to remember that everything is an experience. We can learn from every experience we have and there's no such thing as failure, it's just changing, adapting, and bettering yourself for the future.*

**Royal Bank
of Canada**

Royal Bank of Canada (RBC) is one of Canada's largest banks and a global financial institution with a purpose-driven, principles-led approach to delivering leading performance. For RBC, diversity and inclusion is more than just a value – it's a strength, it's an engine for growth, innovation and prosperity, and above all, it's one of the ways RBC's purpose of helping clients thrive and communities prosper is brought to life. Royal Bank of Canada knows workplaces and communities are stronger when everyone feels respected and empowered, and is committed to driving meaningful change.

Megan Zucker is a Managing Director at RBC Capital Markets with 25+ years of Anti-Money Laundering, Economic Sanctions and Financial Crime experience. *I've discovered that the most joyful state is to not be consumed by external judgment. Being unique, therefore, should trigger feelings of pride rather than shame for anyone. 'The things that make me different make me, me' is a concept that drives us to embrace our differences as a gift.*

Rufaro Chiriseri is an Associate Director and Fixed Income Strategist in RBC Wealth Management London. *There's quite frankly not enough women working in finance, and that needs to change. It's important to bring people to the table with a broad spectrum of experiences, as the solutions to a problem will come from different angles. More importantly, having more diversity in an organisation means that certain issues will not be overlooked. It's so important that you have people from different demographics represented.*

Kelly Coffey
Kelly is only the fourth CEO in City National's 67-year history. Prior to joining City National (City National is a subsidiary of RBC) she served as the Chief Executive Officer of J.P. Morgan's U.S. Private Bank. Kelly was named to *American Banker's list of the 25 Most Powerful Women in Banking* in 2020. *You have to speak up and ask for what you want. Be brave, push yourself, take risks and go for roles that will stretch you. Don't sit back waiting and hoping you will be recognised for your hard work and talent. Make sure your voice is heard.*

ST. JAMES'S PLACE
WEALTH MANAGEMENT

St. James's Place Wealth Management (SJP) puts long term relationships and advice that clients trust at the heart of everything they do. At SJP, the vision is to create a vibrant place to work where difference is recognised as a strength and where talented people can flourish and achieve their highest potential, because people are at the heart of the business and ensuring the creation of equal opportunities and providing clarity of purpose is essential. SJP aims to attract, retain and develop the best people from all walks of life and from all backgrounds, focusing on building a community with equal opportunities where everyone feels valued.

Claire Blackwell is the Director of Marketing at St. James's Place. Claire is responsible for the corporate brand proposition, identity and marketing services provided to Partners of SJP. *You have to expect that you're going to have setbacks regularly in your career. It's about how you deal with those setbacks that's really important. You've got to learn to build resilience, a little bit of a thick skin, some agility, a little bit of grace, and a desire to continuously improve and learn.*

Zohul Malikzada is a fully qualified Financial Advisor, trading as an Associate Partner Practice of St. James's Place. She is passionate about working with women to ensure they have secure financial futures for themselves, their families and their businesses. *We need to see more women in finance. I want more support for women if they choose to work and look after families. Since Covid-19 we can work from home more, but I want that to be the norm. I want people to plan their own work based on family commitments, so that they don't have to sacrifice one for the other.*

Makala Green qualified as the first black female Chartered Financial Planner in the UK and leads a successful Partner Practice at SJP. Makala started her banking career at the age of 16 and progressed through various roles before becoming a qualified financial advisor at 21. *Women bring a completely different edge to the finance industry. I recently became the first black female chartered financial planner in the UK, and that was a monumental achievement. I now use that as a platform to encourage more young females to enter into the financial industry. We still have a long way to go.*

EARNING A WAGE
MEANS THAT YOU HAVE
INDEPENDENCE,
IT MEANS THAT YOU HAVE
OPTIONS,
IT MEANS YOU CAN
PROVIDE FOR YOUR
FAMILY.
IT MEANS THE SAME
FOR WOMEN AS IT MEANS
FOR MEN,
SO PAY US EQUALLY.

VICTORIA DERBYSHIRE

P&G's provides branded products and services of superior quality and value that improve the lives of the world's consumers, now and for generations to come. P&G products combine *'what's needed'* with *'what's possible'*— making laundry rooms, living rooms, bedrooms, kitchens, nurseries and bathrooms a little more enjoyable since 1837. Founded by an Englishman and an Irishman, today P&G is headquartered in Cincinnati, Ohio.

P&G is committed to doing what's right and being a good corporate citizen. Citizenship is built into how P&G does business every day. P&G is focused on being a force for good and a force for growth in each area of its Citizenship work: Community Impact, Equality & Inclusion (E&I) and Environmental Sustainability, all built on a foundation of Ethics & Corporate Responsibility.

P&G believes in E&I and will continue to build a diverse employee and leadership base to reflect the consumers it serves around the world, and to foster an inclusive, respectful, welcoming and affirming culture. P&G aspires to build a better world with equal voice, equal opportunity, and equal representation for everyone, and brings this to life in the four key areas where it can have the greatest impact: with employees, alongside partners, leveraging brands and within communities.

In gender equality, P&G continues to make progress on its aspiration to reach 50/50 representation of women and men at every level of the organisation, and to achieve equitable advancement of multicultural women at every level. P&G remains committed to flexible work, intentional career planning, pay equity and paid parental leave, which are all proven accelerators of gender equality. P&G continues to partner with organisations that help remove barriers to education for girls and create economic opportunities for women, and harnesses the power of its brands to challenge bias and shape culture.

P&G believes it's time for inequality to end, and is committed to being part of the solution with deliberate, sustained action. Unfortunately, far too often, the burden of seeking equality has rested on the shoulders of those most marginalised. P&G is helping to address this by establishing the P&G *Take On Race Fund* to help fuel organisations that fight for justice, advance economic opportunity, enable greater access to education and health care, and make communities more equitable. Internally, P&G is ensuring its policies and practices are not just inclusive, but deliberately advance and enable E&I.

N°7

No7 Beauty Company, part of Walgreens Boots Alliance, is a new and dynamic consumer-led beauty business launched in April 2021 which holds iconic international beauty brands. For 86 years, since No7 launched in 1935, its ambition has been to support and empower people across the world through premium but affordable skincare, with a pledge to put sustainability at the heart of how it does business.

No7 believes in creating beauty for everyone and therefore recognising and celebrating our differences, determined on empowering everyone to bring their authentic selves. The No7 Beauty Company shares a culture where racial diversity, equity and inclusion are embedded in everything, from the way No7 researches and test products, to the ranges produced and how the brands are advertised. No7 knows talented and diverse teams bring new perspectives at all levels and creates conditions where everyone can thrive, and has an inclusive recruitment approach that ensures every shortlist of candidates for interview is diverse and so too are the interview panels used to appoint them.

All of No7's team members spend the equivalent of one day per quarter on learning activities related to diversity, equity and inclusion. With unconscious bias learning for all and training for managers to lead inclusively, the brand makes sure everyone can play an active part in developing its culture.

Through its *Unstoppable Together* platform, No7 is committed to supporting and empowering women to live life on their own terms, helping them overcome barriers and dismantling stereotypes that hold them back. The brand drove important conversations and change through its inaugural *Unstoppable Together* campaign and provided resources and support for women impacted by the *SHEcession*.

ALLEN & OVERY

Allen & Overy is a global law firm that helps the world's leading businesses to grow, innovate and thrive. For almost a century, they have built a reputation for their commitment to think ahead and bring original solutions to their clients' most complex legal and commercial challenges.

To do this, A&O harness their global strength and local knowledge. They drive towards their vision to become the world's most innovative law firm, and will continue to create an environment where the brightest minds can flourish.

Allen & Overy believes the world needs different. It's by bringing together varied lived experiences, perspectives and thoughts that we generate ideas and build creative solutions. We all thrive when what makes us different is embraced. A&O knows it can't be advanced as a firm by being the same, which is why diversity and inclusion is one of their strategic priorities.

Allen & Overy is committed to supporting a culture that drives diversity and inclusion and to create an environment where everyone feels that they can bring their authentic selves to work. To feel like they belong. To be All In.

By continually listening using tools such as focus groups and surveys, alongside input from its affinity groups, A&O understand the wide range of experiences and barriers that diverse colleagues face. They hold themselves accountable, with data and transparency at the heart of their strategy. This enables A&O to both measure progress and be honest when the progress is not what it should be.

Allen & Overy's commitment extends beyond its own walls, utilising its expertise on a wide range of global issues in collaboration with clients and other organisations.

General Mills

General Mills is a leading global food company whose purpose is to *'make food the world loves'*. Its portfolio of beloved brands includes names such as Cheerios, Nature Valley, Blue Buffalo, Häagen-Dazs, Old El Paso, Pillsbury, Betty Crocker, Yoplait, Annie's and more.

At General Mills, there is strength and opportunity in diversity – throughout the company, within our communities, and amongst consumers. Building a culture of belonging is an imperative business strategy for General Mills as it not only accelerates growth, but champions the voices of those with different backgrounds, experiences and approaches. In doing so, the company produces greater levels of creativity and innovative thought that ultimately drives performance.

General Mills creates a seat at the table for all employees by fostering a safe, inclusive and rewarding workplace, and seeks to make a positive impact with its people and its communities. Inclusion at General Mills is embedded into four pillars: workforce, cultural, consumer and societal. Each pillar serves to inform and elevate the others for the greatest impact on the company and world.

General Mills is founded on the idea that diversity and inclusion is not just the right thing to do, but because their more than 100 consumer brands are produced and marketed in more than 100 countries on six continents, it's critical that their teams and suppliers represent the wide expanse of people served— especially given the cultural nature of food.

With a leadership team comprised of women and men, leaders born outside the US, leaders who have spent their careers at General Mills and those who are very new to the company, the business is committed to embracing and encouraging the exchange of ideas, in a safe and respectful environment.

Kimberly-Clark

Kimberly-Clark is a global company focused on providing Better Care for a Better World through product innovation and building personal care, consumer tissue and K-C Professional brands.

Kimberly-Clark and its trusted brands are an indispensable part of life for people in more than 175 countries. With approximately 46,000 employees worldwide and operations in 34 countries, the company is fueled by ingenuity, creativity, and an understanding of people's most essential needs, creating products that help individuals experience more of what's important to them. Kimberly-Clark's success lies in having built an inclusive global organisation that applies the diverse experiences and passions of its people to brands that make life better for people around the world. The company has a variety of employee resource groups that aim to foster a greater understanding of different perspectives and backgrounds through cultural events and panel discussions.

Kimberly-Clark also continuously works to foster an environment where the employees – and the broad perspectives they bring to work – allow them to make better business decisions, create innovative products and enhance the experiences of consumers around the world. Additionally, with a Non-Discrimination Policy that recognises that talent and skills are not defined by race, colour, religion, sex/gender, age, sexual orientation, national origin, disability, gender identity, genetic information, veteran status, education or background, Kimberly-Clark's Human Rights in Employment Policy prohibits discrimination and/or harassment based on these factors and any other categories protected by applicable law.

Kimberly-Clark is committed to building a workforce that reflects its consumers and unleashing the power of its people – where all are inspired to do their best work and differences are valued and essential for success.

BT is one of the world's leading communications services companies providing solutions for customers in over 180 countries.

BT's purpose is as simple as it is ambitious: we connect for good. There are no limits to what people can do when they connect.
BT's ambition is to be the world's most trusted connector of people, devices and machines. Technology is rapidly and fundamentally changing our lives, businesses and societies, and trust will play a critical part in our customers being able to take advantage of these changes.

Internally, BT is building a culture where people can be their best, stripping away complexity and giving colleagues the chance to learn and grow. BT wants to be a destination employer that attracts and retains a diverse and talented mix of colleagues who are able to focus on what's important to customers. All employees are able to connect through BT's people networks. Everyone can join BT's gender equality, ethnicity, LGBT+, ability, faith and carers' networks which offer support and let the business know what's important to them so BT can improve and develop the whole business.

BT knows it's crucial that employees reflect the diversity of its customers from around the world and having people from all walks of life makes a more creative and innovative company. That variety of experience, culture and background allows teams to truly use the power of communication to make a better world, giving everyone products and services which actually make a difference in their lives.

BT also works to help reduce inequality by supporting women in the digital workplace. BT *Skills for Tomorrow* aims to empower 25 million people by giving them the skills they need to make the most of life in a digital world.

Founded in 1891, Hormel Foods is still proudly based in Austin, Minnesota, and rooted in the values on which it was founded — integrity, an uninterrupted quest for quality and innovation, a respect for one another and a commitment to community. Hormel Foods believes that good business and good stewardship go hand in hand. Hormel Foods invests in its people and partners, aims to improve communities and the world, and to create products that improve the lives of others. For nearly 130 years, Hormel Foods has developed a team-oriented culture to drive results. Indeed, the cornerstone of the company is the inspired team: the dedicated employees who are committed to delivering consistent results. Hormel Foods is actively implementing initiatives to encourage diversity and inclusion of people, thoughts and experiences to further enhance the capabilities of the team.

Hormel Foods embraces inclusion and diversity because of its belief that it makes for a better company. Diversity relates to those aspects of ourselves that make us unique. Inclusion refers to an environment that supports and nurtures that individuality and allows it to grow and prosper. Diversity is a given because everyone is different. Inclusiveness is the journey that Hormel Foods happily embraces. It's important because their workforce and their consumers are changing. So Hormel Foods is working every day to create an environment where all employees feel as if they belong within their culture and still are valued for their individuality, valuing the similarities and differences they all share. Valuing differences allows people to be more creative and innovative. Hormel Foods desires an environment filled with unique perspectives in which people feel challenged and excited coming to work every day, and where they aspire to remain. Hormel Foods is aiming to create a workplace where people feel free to bring their whole selves to work.

XP Inc. – the leading financial services platform in Brazil has the purpose of transforming the financial market in order to improve people's lives. It is committed to promoting a culture of gender equality, women's empowerment and inclusion. In 2020, XP Inc. declared its public commitment to achieve at least 50% of women in its workforce by 2025. The initiative is part of the MLHR3, a collective movement dedicated to accelerating women's inclusion in the financial sector. Created in 2020, MLHR3 joins more than 300 XP Inc. professionals committed to gender equality and has an open communication channel with Thiago Maffra, XP Inc. CEO.

There is still a long journey ahead, but XP Inc. strongly believes in and works towards an increasingly inclusive ecosystem with equality for all women.

ACKNOWLEDGEMENTS

I would like to thank the following people for inspiration, connectivity and masses of practical help;

For bringing the book and films to life
Sane Seven, *Photographer*
Lauren Lind, *Film-maker*
Bea Appleby, *Editor*
Prof Phil Cleaver, *Designer*
Callum Blake, *Illustrator*
Eilidh Doig, *Assistant Designer*
Hester Lacey, *Journalist*
Geraldine Bedell, *Journalist*
Rosanna Greenstreet, *Journalist*
Jessica Mangaba, *Photographer, Brazil*
Linha de Pensamento Produtora, *Videographer, Brazil*
Mariana Romão, *Interviewer, Brazil*
Laura Whiteside, *Research & Foundation Manager*
Becky Small, *Campaign Manager*
Holly Droy, *Content Creator*
Veryan Dexter, *Research*
Helen Jordan, *Data Scientist*
Imogen Stoddart, *Photoshoot Producer*
Scarlett Burton, *Hair & Makeup*
Rachel Shepherd, *Hair & Makeup*

For helping us to connect in the UK and USA
Central Talent Booking
Rosemary Reed
WOW Foundation
Dame Hazel Genn

For helping us to connect in Brazil
Sandra di Moise
Angela Donaggio
Claudia Pagnano

Every woman in the book was interviewed on film and these can all be seen at

www.thefemalelead.com